THE MANNERHEIM LINE 1920–39

Finnish Fortifications of the Winter War

BAIR IRINCHEEV

ILLUSTRATED BY BRIAN DELF

Series editors Marcus Cowper and Nikolai Bogdanovic

First published in 2009 by Osprey Publishing
Midland House, West Way, Botley, Oxford OX2 0PH, UK
443 Park Avenue South, New York, NY 10016, USA
E-mail: info@ospreypublishing.com

ISBN: 978 1 84603 384 1
E-book ISBN: 978 1 84908 100 9

Editorial by Ilios Publishing Ltd, Oxford, UK (www.iliospublishing.com)
Cartography: Map Studio, Romsey, UK
Page layout by Ken Vail Graphic Design, Cambridge, UK (kvgd.com)
Typeset in Myriad Pro and Sabon
Index by Alison Worthington
Originated by PPS Grasmere, Leeds, UK
Printed in China through Bookbuilders

09 10 11 12 13   10 9 8 7 6 5 4 3 2 1

A CIP catalogue record for this book is available from the British Library.

ARTIST'S NOTE

Readers may care to note that the original paintings from which the
colour plates in this book were prepared are available for private sale.
All reproduction copyright whatsoever is retained by the Publishers.
All enquiries should be addressed to:

Brian Delf, 7 Burcot Park, Burcot, Abingdon, OX14 3DH, UK

The Publishers regret that they can enter into no correspondence
upon this matter.

THE FORTRESS STUDY GROUP (FSG)

The object of the FSG is to advance the education of the public in the
study of all aspects of fortifications and their armaments, especially
works constructed to mount or resist artillery. The FSG holds an annual
conference in September over a long weekend with visits and evening
lectures, an annual tour abroad lasting about eight days, and an annual
Members' Day.

The FSG journal FORT is published annually, and its newsletter Casemate
is published three times a year. Membership is international. For further
details, please contact:

The Secretary, c/o 6 Lanark Place, London W9 1BS, UK

Website: www.fsgfort.com

THE WOODLAND TRUST

Osprey Publishing are supporting the Woodland Trust, the UK's leading
woodland conservation charity, by funding the dedication of trees.

GLOSSARY

Anti-tank rock barrier	The most common type of obstacle for stopping tanks on the Mannerheim Line. Consisted of 4–12 rows of granite rocks.
Anti-turret barrier	A barrier made of logs attached to strong trees in a forest at the height of a tank's turret. Could cause damage to a main gun or turret if a tank drove into it at high speed.
Armoured bunker	A bunker on the Mannerheim Line that had its frontal wall or frontal wall and roof made of armoured plates.
Armoured tower/cupola	Installed in roofs of cannon forts and new bunkers of the Mannerheim Line. Had six slits for observation and close-range combat.
Casemate	On the Mannerheim Line, part of the bunker where weapons are installed, or a concrete bunker in general.
Commander	The Red Army abolished officer ranks and introduced another name for commissioned officers during the Russian Civil War. All officers were renamed commanders. The word 'officer' only came back into use in the Red Army in 1943.
Cuckoo	A Red Army nickname for a Finnish sniper.
Death bunker, or death dugout	Accommodation dugout of the 2nd Heavy Artillery Battalion in Lähde. 32 Finnish artillerymen were killed inside the dugout on 13 February 1940.
lines	A Finnish female name, the nickname of bunker No. 17 in Summankylä area.
Karelian sculptor	Nickname for a heavy Red Army cannon firing at Finnish bunkers over open sights.
Kombrig	A rank in the Red Army in 1939–40, equivalent to a general-major.
Korsu:	A Finnish term for any type of bunker: concrete, wooden, with machine guns or without. The loose use of this term in Finnish archive sources and literature causes a lot of confusion.
LBT, Lichny Tank Boitsa (trooper's own tank)	A nickname for an armoured shield on skis designed to provide cover from 7.62mm ammunition during an approach to the bunkers. About 50,000 such shields were issued to the troops of the Red Army in the Winter War.
Millionaire	Official name of bunker No. 5 in the Lähde sector. The name was given to the bunker due to its extremely high cost of construction. The Red Army used the name Millionaire to designate all the large bunkers on the Mannerheim Line.
Peltola	The name of a house next to which bunker No. 11 in Summankylä sector was located. The bunker was named after the house.
Poppius	2nd Lieutenant Poppius was the first commander of bunker No. 4 in the Lähde sector. During the Winter War the bunker retained the name of its first commander.
Stalin's sledgehammer	A nickname for a heavy Red Army cannon firing at Finnish bunkers over open sights.
Strongpoint	In the Finnish army, a fortified position of an infantry platoon, often built for all-round defence and featuring extensive use of flanking fire.
Terttu	Finnish female name, and the nickname of bunker No. 2 in the Summankylä sector.
Torsu	Finnish nickname for the command bunker of the Lähde sector.
Viipuri	The Finnish name for the capital of Karelia and the main city on the Karelian Isthmus.
Vyborg	The Swedish and Russian name for Viipuri.

FOR A CATALOGUE OF ALL BOOKS PUBLISHED BY OSPREY MILITARY
AND AVIATION PLEASE CONTACT:

Osprey Direct, c/o Random House Distribution Center,
400 Hahn Road, Westminster, MD 21157
E-mail: uscustomerservice@ospreypublishing.com

Osprey Direct, The Book Service Ltd, Distribution Centre,
Colchester Road, Frating Green, Colchester, Essex, CO7 7DW
E-mail: customerservice@ospreypublishing.com

www.ospreypublishing.com

CONTENTS

THE MANNERHEIM LINE 1920–39

FINNISH FORTIFICATIONS ON THE KARELIAN ISTHMUS

INTRODUCTION

The Mannerheim Line, the system of Finnish fortifications on the Karelian Isthmus, became legendary during the Winter War of 1939–40, when it was tested in battle and finally fell to the steamroller of the Red Army offensive. Built in the 1920s and the 1930s, this line of defences stretched from the Gulf of Finland in the west to Lake Ladoga in the east, thus covering the entire Karelian Isthmus, a strategically important sector of the Soviet–Finnish border. The design, development, defence and destruction of the Mannerheim Line make for a fascinating study, not only due to the vast variety of fortification solutions employed in it, but also because of the battles fought over its bunkers and trenches.

The historical background

Prior to the Winter War, Finland had had a long history of wars, conflicts and border changes. This can be explained by its location between two larger rival states, the Russian empire (later the USSR, now the Russian Federation) and Sweden. During the Middle Ages and the early modern period, Finland, then a province of Sweden, witnessed wars on a regular basis. In 1809, after yet another war between Sweden and Russia, the latter emerged victorious and took control over the whole of Finland as a prize. In 1917, after the collapse of the Russian empire, Finland became an independent state for the first time in its history. After a short but bloody civil war in 1918, the country began a process of peaceful development. A peace treaty with Soviet Russia was signed in Tartu, Estonia, in 1920. The nascent Soviet republic was still suffering the effects of the Civil War and the terms of the peace treaty were quite favourable for Finland; on the Karelian Isthmus the border was set at the Sister River, the former administrative border between the Grand Duchy of Finland and the province of St Petersburg. At the closest point the border was only 32 kilometres from Petrograd (renamed Leningrad in 1924), the second largest city of Soviet Russia with a population of 3.19 million people as of 1939, and an important military and industrial centre. For Finland, the Karelian Isthmus, the new border area, was also strategically important. The isthmus comprises a stretch of land between the Gulf of Finland in the west and Lake Ladoga in the east. This area provided the shortest route into the heart of Finland and to the Finnish capital Helsinki. A relatively good road and railway network and the absence of any significant natural obstacles made the terrain even more inviting for potential attackers. The area has been described by Finnish historians and the media as the 'key to Finland'.

The Karelian Isthmus was also of great strategic importance to the Soviet Union. The border between Finland and Soviet Russia was only some 30 kilometres from Leningrad at its closest point. The city was home to vitally important military production factories and was also a key base for the Baltic Red Banner Fleet.

Owing to ideological differences, recent domination in the imperial period, and the fresh scars of the Finnish civil war, in which Soviet Russia secretly supported the Finnish Red Guards, both national governments treated each other with great distrust and suspicion. The Finnish leaders thought (as history correctly showed) that Russia would at some point make a comeback as a superpower and try to incorporate Finland into its realm again. The Soviet leaders viewed officially neutral Finland as a hostile, capitalist state. Its territory, and especially the Karelian Isthmus, could be used by a European state (be it France, England, Poland or Germany) as a jumping-off position to assault Leningrad. As the distance from the Finnish border to Leningrad was 30–50 kilometres, the Soviet leaders viewed the north-western borders of the USSR as extremely vulnerable.

Both countries began fortifying the new border almost immediately after signing the peace treaty in 1920. The line of Soviet fortifications south of the border was named the *KaUR*, the Karelian Fortified Region. The Finnish line of defences was named the Main Defence Line. Later it was dubbed the Mannerheim Line, although it is important to note that this name was given to it by foreign reporters, not by the Finnish Army. It should be noted that there is also a common misunderstanding in Russia and in Finland about this term. For Finns the Mannerheim Line is the line of defences, where the Red Army advance was stopped in mid-December 1939; for the Russians, however, the Mannerheim Line is the entire complex of Finnish fortifications on the Karelian Isthmus.

CHRONOLOGY

1917	25 October	Communist revolution takes place in Russia.
	6 December	Finland declares independence from Russia.
1920	14 October	Finland and Soviet Russia sign the peace treaty of Tartu.
1920s		Construction of the first Finnish defensive lines.
1930s		Modernization of fortifications on the Karelian Isthmus.
1939	June–August	Volunteers from all over Finland take part in fortification work on the Karelian Isthmus.
	23 August	The Molotov–Ribbentrop Pact is signed in Moscow.
	1 September	Germany invades Poland.

LEFT
A poor quality picture of a Mannerheim Line bunker from the 1920s, taken by a Soviet spy on a miniature camera. The picture shows how clearly the bunkers stood out from the surrounding terrain. (Antero Uitto)

RIGHT
Noisniemi artillery fort on the Vuoksi River, photographed by a Soviet spy in the late 1920s–early 1930s. A map and photo album of Finnish fortifications on the Karelian Isthmus was produced by the Red Army Central Intelligence Bureau in the USSR in 1937. However, by 1939 the album was obsolete, as the Finns had built many more bunkers between 1937 and 1939. (Antero Uitto)

The defences of the Karelian Isthmus in 1939

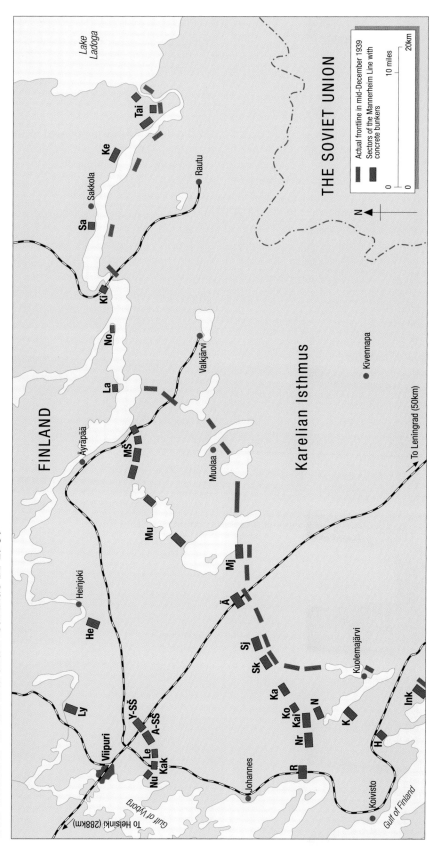

	17 September	The Soviet Union invades Poland.
	October– November	Several rounds of negotiations between the USSR and Finland take place about the border on the Karelian Isthmus, but each ends in a failure to agree.
	26 November	The Mainila incident, which serves as *casus belli* for the Soviet invasion, takes place.
	29 November	The USSR breaks off diplomatic relations with Finland.
	30 November	The USSR invades Finland, without any formal declaration of war.
	17–23 December	The first Soviet offensive against the Mannerheim Line fails.
	23 December	A Finnish counteroffensive on the Karelian Isthmus fails.
	24–27 December	A renewed Soviet offensive on the Karelian Isthmus fails.
1940	January	The Red Army prepares for a new, massive offensive against the Mannerheim Line.
1940	1–3 February	First reconnaissance in force against the Mannerheim Line takes place. Battle of Sk2 'Terttu' bunker in the Summa village sector. The Sk1 and Sk2 bunkers are captured by the 355th Rifle Regiment.
	11 February	The grand offensive of the Red Army starts. Breakthrough in the Lähde sector. The Sj4 Poppius bunker is captured.
	13 February	The Sj5 Millionaire bunker is captured.
	15 February	At 15.00 hrs the Finnish commander-in-chief Marshal Mannerheim orders his troops to fall back to the Intermediary Line.
	20–28 February	Battles in the Salmenkaita sector.
	17–28 February	Battles in the Muolaa sector.
	28 February	The Finns abandon the Intermediary Line in the afternoon.
	1–13 March	The Red Army units cross the Gulf of Vyborg and threaten to encircle Vyborg.
	12 March	An armistice is signed in Moscow by the Finnish and Soviet delegations.
	13 March	At noon, Moscow time, the armistice comes into effect. All military activity on the Karelian Isthmus is halted. Finland cedes the Karelian Isthmus to the USSR.
	Summer	All the remaining bunkers of the Mannerheim Line are destroyed by Red Army sappers. The Finns commence construction of a new fortified line, called the Salpa Line, along the new border with the USSR. In similar fashion, construction work begins on the Harparskog Line on the Hanko Peninsula, which has been rented to the USSR by Finland for 30 years for use as a naval base.

DESIGN AND DEVELOPMENT

The first fortifications

After discussions and deliberations during the early years of Finnish independence, the Main Defence Line of Finland on the Karelian Isthmus was set to run from west to east through Römpötti, Karhula, Summa, Leipäsuo, Muolaa, and Salmenkaita and then along the northern bank of the Vuoksi River and Lake Suvanto. The line of defence fully utilized terrain features, defending the most crucial highways and railways, and paying particular attention to areas that tanks could easily move in.

The first fortifications were modest in size but vast in number. The most typical fortification during this initial period of construction were frontal-firing concrete bunkers with one heavy machine gun emplaced. The bunkers lacked ventilation systems, periscopes, special machine-gun mounts, and sometimes even doors, and were often built using poor-quality concrete. The only steel reinforcements provided were H-shaped steel bars in the roofs of the bunkers. Such fortifications were built in the most vulnerable areas, usually next to main roads and railways, and were built to maximize the natural defensive features of the terrain, using small rivers and brooks as obstacle lines. The bunkers were quite tall and stood out clearly in the surrounding terrain. To make things worse, the bunkers were not guarded or camouflaged during peacetime, which gave Soviet spies a perfect chance to map them and even take pictures of them without any danger of being caught. In addition to these fortifications, concrete shelters and small concrete trenches were built.

In general, the fortifications erected during the 1920s were of poor quality and were built to a low budget. However, one exception to this rule was the group of formidable cannon forts built along the northern bank of the Vuoksi River and Lake Suvanto. Each fort had four cannons or machine guns, with two of them providing a superb field of flanking fire in each direction. For observation and close defence each fort was equipped with an armoured tower. The guns installed were either Meller or Nordenfeldt cannons of 2–3-inch calibre. A total of six such forts was built on the Lauttaniemi, Noisniemi, Kiviniemi, Hoviniemi (at Sakkola village), Kekkiniemi and Patoniemi headlands. The bunkers were built into the sandy hillsides in such a way that they were virtually invisible from the other side of the lake – the direction from which any attacker would approach.

The Finnish defences on the Karelian Isthmus were anchored on coastal batteries and forts in the Gulf of Finland and Lake Ladoga. Some of these fortifications were inherited from the Russian empire, whilst others were built in the 1920s and 1930s. The most important batteries were Kaarnajoki (containing four 6-inch cannons) and Järisevä (containing two 120mm cannons) behind the Taipale sector on Lake Ladoga, the Koivisto archipelago batteries (containing six 10-inch cannons and two 6-inch cannons), Humaljoki fort (containing eight 6-inch cannons and four 57mm cannons), Tuppura fort (containing four 6-inch cannons and two 57mm cannons) and the Ristiniemi battery (containing two 10-inch cannons) in the Gulf of Finland.

The modernizations of the 1930s

In the 1930s, as the world situation became more and more unstable, the process of fortification of the Karelian Isthmus resumed. New types of bunkers were developed and built, including the so-called 'Millionaire' bunkers. The main features of the new construction period were the modernization and strengthening of the existing machine-gun bunkers, the completion of

A gun-port for close-range combat in the Sk5 bunker, suited to a Suomi sub-machine gun or a Lahti-Saloranta light machine gun. (Bair Irincheev)

unfinished bunkers in the Inkilä sector, and the construction of some new bunkers that were of a completely different design. However, modernization of the Main Defence Line had not been completed by the beginning of hostilities between the USSR and Finland.

A unique test bunker was built in the Lähde sector, comprising a long wall of reinforced concrete with different degrees of reinforcement within the concrete. The bunker was then subjected to test-firing by heavy Finnish artillery and the most durable combination of concrete and reinforcement was selected for use in future fortification projects. At the same time, the effects of employing protective armoured plate at different angles were explored, leading to further crucial decisions on the design of the new bunkers.

The existing machine-gun bunkers were modernized in the following ways. The walls and roofs were thickened with reinforcement added to the concrete. Additional chambers were built so that the direction of fire could be changed from frontal to flanking. Also, some bunkers were transformed into shelters, and others had armoured towers added to them.

The new, massive bunkers built consisted of an underground shelter (located at a depth of 2–4m) which could house 20–40 men and two to three casemates. However, such structures were extremely costly and only a few of them were built.

It is important to note that there was no absolutely standard design for these formidable fortifications, as each bunker was built to fit the unique features of the terrain. However, all bunkers featured certain standardized elements of design, and standard weapons.

A THE SJ5 'MILLIONAIRE' MACHINE-GUN BUNKER

The Sj5 'Millionaire' (in Finnish, *Miljoonalinnake*) bunker was the most famous of all the fortifications of the Mannerheim Line. This reconstruction is the first ever to be attempted of the whole site around the bunker. The bunker was about 60m long, and was equipped with four heavy machine guns set up for flanking fire, and had three armoured towers for observation and close combat. It could accommodate 20–40 men in the underground shelters, and had three casemates. This bunker was built between 1937 and 1939, as part of the last efforts to strengthen the defences of the isthmus. The bunker is shown as per December 1939, before the fighting in this sector.

The SJ5 'Millionaire' machine-gun bunker

An intact armoured tower on a Finnish bunker. Note the protection for shell splinters on the observation and close-range defence slits. (Carl-Fredrik Geust)

BELOW
The standard air ventilation system of a Finnish bunker. A handle for circulating the air can be seen in the lower part of the picture. (Carl-Fredrik Geust)

The weapons of the Mannerheim Line

The main weapon emplaced in the bunkers was a heavy Maxim machine gun, set on a specially built wooden carriage. In some cases the wooden carriage was built with haste and machine guns were attached to it with leather belts. The thick walls of the bunker and the small size of the gun-ports often silenced, or deflected, the sound of the machine gun firing. The machine guns were attached to the water supply system of the bunkers to allow the circulation of water inside the weapon's cooling sleeve.

A special version of the Suomi sub-machine gun was developed for use inside the tower; the long wooden stock of the original Suomi was removed and a pistol-type handle was attached to it instead. A special narrow muzzle brake was attached to the cooling sleeve on the barrel so that the gun could be fired through the observation slits.

The bunkers were also equipped with additional gun-ports for close combat. Normally, a small shelf was built into the wall of the bunker under such gun-ports, to hold several clips or ammunition drums. Defenders could use rifles, Suomi sub-machine guns or Lahti-Saloranta light machine guns for firing from these gun-ports.

The preferred anti-tank weapon of the Mannerheim Line defenders was the 37mm Bofors anti-tank gun, either purchased from Sweden or produced in Finland under licence. The cannon was capable of penetrating the armour of all Soviet tanks, except for new top-secret heavy tanks, which were deployed in the Summa village sector in December 1939. However, the weapons were so scarce that a Finnish battalion on the Mannerheim Line would only deploy one or two such guns for the whole sector of defence. Due to the scarcity of these anti-tank weapons, crews had to build several positions for their guns and be ready to move them in the course of a battle.

The inadequacy of anti-tank defences on the Line spurred the defenders into improvising anti-tank weapons for close-quarters combat. These included petrol bombs, satchel charges and even shotguns for firing at the observation slits of Soviet tanks at point-blank range. Petrol bombs, dubbed 'Molotov cocktails' (to mock the Soviet foreign minister, who was seen in Finland as one of the architects of the Soviet invasion), became a legend of the Winter War. Initially they were improvised weapons made at the front, but later in the war the State Alcohol Factory in Rajamäki, Finland began mass production of these using cognac and vodka bottles. Recent battlefield finds suggest that even Viipuri's Brewery was engaged in making Molotov cocktails, filling lemonade bottles with flammable liquid.

Standard elements of bunker design
Machine guns were installed in casemates for flanking fire, but this left the bunker exposed to attacks from the front. In order to solve this problem,

BELOW LEFT
Bunk beds inside a 'Millionaire'-type Finnish bunker, probably Sk10 'The Ten'. Note the straw mattresses and the hooks for hanging uniforms.
(Carl-Fredrik Geust)

BELOW RIGHT
A stove for heating and cooking food inside a bunker, most likely Sk10 'The Ten'.
(Carl-Fredrik Geust)

The badly damaged frontal armoured wall of a Finnish armoured bunker, probably Le6 or Le7. Note the two wide observation slits and the narrower gun-port below them. (Carl-Fredrik Geust)

armoured towers with slits for observation and for engaging in close-range combat were built into the roofs of the casemates. The towers had armoured walls with a thickness of 12–20cm and six observation slits. The slits could be closed by rotating an armoured ring inside the bunker. There was a hatch at the bottom of the tower and a ladder provided access into the casemate of the bunker. Finnish officers described the tower as a 'steel cup, large enough to fit two people in it, that was installed upside down onto the roof of the bunker'. An armoured tower was quite low and only protruded 30-40 centimetres above the roof of the bunker. Observation slits were almost at the same level with the roof of the bunker. The towers were primarily used by artillery observers and duty observers from the bunker's garrison. Although the towers were low, they were the only element of the bunker visible from the Red Army's side, and were thus subjected to accurate artillery fire, often over open sights.

Most of the bunkers were gas-proof in case chemical weapons were used by the enemy. The ventilation system of the bunkers comprised a large milk-churning-type machine that was operated manually. When a large number of soldiers slept inside the bunker, they had to operate the ventilation system several times during the night, as oxygen would run low in this sealed environment.

The accommodation chambers of the bunker were equipped with bi-level bunk beds, placed along the walls of the underground passages. The frames of the beds were metal with wooden slats, and the mattresses were filled with straw or hay. Small shelves were installed along the walls for the soldiers' small personal items, like canteens and water bottles.

B   A MACHINE-GUN BUNKER IN THE HUMALJOKI SECTOR, ON THE TERIJOKI–KOIVISTO RAILWAY

This type of bunker was the most prevalent among the defences of the Mannerheim Line. The bunker was located to the west of the Terijoki–Koivisto railway line, and was made of concrete. Its weaponry comprised one Maxim heavy machine gun, mounted on a standard Finnish Army tripod. The latter was placed directly onto a concrete shelf below the embrasure. It appears that the bunkers did not even have any doors on them. In 1939 these bunkers were mostly obsolete, and being clearly visible in the terrain they fell easy prey to Soviet artillery.

A machine-gun bunker in the Humaljoki sector, on the Terijoki–Koivisto railway

RIGHT
A Finnish wooden bunker
destroyed by a direct hit
from Soviet heavy artillery,
in an unknown sector of
the Mannerheim Line.
(Carl-Fredrik Geust)

BELOW
A Soviet prisoner of war with
some bread given to him by
Finnish soldiers, inside a Finnish
wooden bunker in Summa,
January 1940. (Bair Irincheev)

The bunkers were heated by means of pre-installed stoves made of brick. The chimneys were thin and long, in order to conceal the exiting smoke, and were protected by a layer of concrete about 40cm thick. A bunker normally had a built-in well or two to supply water for cooling the machine guns and for potable water for the garrison.

The bunkers were connected to the battalion's headquarters by an underground phone cable laid at a depth of two metres, which proved to be quite inadequate during the heavy artillery barrages laid down by Soviet artillery. Some bunkers had radio sets brought into them by artillery observation teams. However, it is important to note that these radio sets were not pre-installed inside the bunkers. When phone lines were damaged by artillery fire, the garrisons of the bunkers had to rely on runners for the transfer of messages.

Most of the bunkers were built of reinforced concrete; however, the Russian Imperial Navy left behind plenty of armoured plates for the repair of its battleships in Finland, and so the Finnish Army decided to use them for bunker construction. Live artillery test-firing at the bunker in Lähde confirmed that a sloping 30cm-thick armour plate provided a level of protection comparable with 1.5m of reinforced concrete. This gave Finnish Army engineers the idea of building bunkers with the frontal wall and roof of the casemates protected by armour plates. The casemates were very compact, low and easy to conceal in the surrounding terrain. The best example of this is the Ink6 bunker, which stands only a metre or so above the ground and blends completely into the hillock on which it was built. The gun-ports of these armoured bunkers measured 3cm × 10cm, which allowed only a limited, 60-degree angle of fire. The frontal wall of the bunkers was built at an angle to help deflect incoming artillery rounds. During the course of the fighting this led to the myth that the bunkers were covered with a thick layer of rubber, which caused incoming rounds to ricochet off. The frontal walls and roofs were built of several consecutive layers of armoured plates, each 3–10cm thick, attached to the concrete sidewalls by large bolts. The Soviet war correspondent Sobolev described the armoured casemates of the Ink6 bunker as 'the turrets of a battleship, buried in the ground'.

Again, there was no standard design for the armoured bunkers. The Ink6, Sk10 ('The Ten') and Sj4 'Poppius' bunkers had casemates with roofs and frontal walls of armour plate, while the Le6 and Le7 bunkers had only their frontal walls built of this. The Ink1, Ink3, Ink4, Ink5 and Ink7 bunkers had their casemate walls built of armour plate too.

Just before the outbreak of the Winter War, the Finnish Army decided to change the bunker design once again, primarily due to the high cost of construction of the 'Millionaire' bunkers. Smaller machine-gun bunkers for one or two heavy machine guns without integrated deep underground shelters were built in the Muolaa and Salmenkaita sectors. Each bunker had enough bunk beds to accommodate only 6 to 10 soldiers. Larger concrete shelters were built some 150–200m to the rear of the machine-gun bunkers, and were connected to them by a communication trench. The concrete shelters had only a slightly lower profile than the machine-gun bunkers, and some of them were equipped with armoured towers (for example, shelter No. 37 in the Salmenkaita sector). Building a pair of smaller bunkers without a massive underground gallery at a depth of four metres was a cost-saving solution, and the military value of these machine-gun bunkers was the same as that of the 'Millionaire' bunkers. It is important to note that in both the Salmenkaita and Muolaa sectors the concrete shelters were built only in isolated locations, as the outbreak of hostilities soon halted all work.

A barbed-wire obstacle line in an unknown sector of the Mannerheim Line. (Carl-Fredrik Geust)

In addition to the concrete shelters, numerous wooden bunkers and improvised concrete, iron and combined bunkers were constructed between October and November 1939 after the Finnish Army took up defensive positions on the Karelian Isthmus. The variation in their design was limited only by the available construction materials and the imagination of the builders. Although the Finnish Army had created a clear guide to fortification in the form of a manual, the Finnish officers and soldiers at the front cared little for these strict rules and instead opted for effectiveness.

The cannon forts at Lake Suvanto and the Vuoksi River were armed with Meller and Nordenfeldt 2- or 3-inch fortress cannons, left behind by the Russian Imperial Army after the collapse of the Russian empire. The Meller gun had no recoil system and had an effective range of up to 3,000m, while the Nordenfeldt cannon had range of up to 9,000m and a theoretical rate of fire of up to 20 shots per minute.

The coastal batteries and artillery forts in the Gulf of Finland, the Gulf of Vyborg and around the shores of Lake Ladoga were armed with a variety of World War I-era 5-, 6- and even 10-inch cannon left behind by the Russian Imperial Army or purchased in Europe in the 1920s and 1930s. The most crucial batteries were those of Kaarnajoki in the Taipale sector, armed with four Russian-built Canet 6-inch cannon, and the 10-inch battery on the Koivisto archipelago.

FIELD FORTIFICATIONS ON THE MANNERHEIM LINE

Trenches

Many trenches had been dug in the build-up to the outbreak of hostilities, in October and November 1939. A Finnish battle trench would be about 2m deep, with a step for firing and individual positions for riflemen and machine-gun crews, and the sides revetted with wooden beams. Niches for ammunition were built into the front walls. Foxholes began to appear in the front walls of trenches when war broke out, as the full devastating effect of Soviet artillery fire took its toll on the defenders.

In swampy sectors, like Merkki, Taasionlammet and Munasuo, where digging down was not possible, trenches had to be built on top of the boggy ground. They consisted of two earth walls, strengthened with logs.

A barbed-wire obstacle line, attached to steel poles, combined with an anti-tank rock barrier. The second row of barbed wire can be seen in the distance. The dark object in the background is the Sj5 'Millionaire' bunker. The photo was taken in the Lähde sector of the Mannerheim Line. (Carl-Fredrik Geust)

A modern view of a barbed-wire obstacle attached directly to trees, in the Inkilä sector of the Mannerheim Line. In the 60 years since the war ended, the barbed wire has grown into the trees. (Bair Irincheev)

A trench network normally consisted of platoon strongpoints, and offered the possibility of flanking fire and an all-round defence in case of an enemy breakthrough. Communication trenches and flanking positions were also present.

During the battles on the Mannerheim Line, when Soviet artillery pounded the Finnish defences with up to 12,000 shells per day, most of the trenches were destroyed or filled in by earth and debris. It took a superhuman effort by the Finnish sappers to maintain the trenches in a battleworthy condition, rebuilding them every night in the bitter cold.

Finnish trenches often had armoured shields installed on the breastworks to protect individual riflemen from enemy fire. The shields were rectangular with a gun-port and a thin roof plate, and were thick enough to protect a defender from a standard rifle bullet and shrapnel. However, they could not stop armour-piercing rifle bullets, and during the battles that developed Soviet tanks would target any individual riflemen spotted, firing their main guns at the armoured shield. Thus, in the later battles the Finnish infantry moved between firing positions as quickly as they could in order not to be targeted by Soviet armour.

Wooden bunkers

Wooden bunkers, built both as shelters and as machine-gun positions, were abundant along the Mannerheim Line. The Finnish infantry built them both for accommodation and for strengthening gaps in the Line, the relevant sections being anchored on concrete bunkers. These bunkers varied in size, construction materials and design. In general, although fortification manuals were always close at hand, the Finns preferred to use common sense and constructed bunkers according to the specific terrain features, the available construction materials and the proximity of water sources.

In general, according to the Finnish field manuals, a wooden accommodation bunker for a platoon was to be constructed at a depth of 8m, with two entrances, a ventilation system and heating. Both rocks and soil were to be used on the roof. According to the calculations of Finnish sappers, such a depth would give a bunker adequate protection from enemy 6-inch artillery rounds. In reality very few bunkers were built at such a depth, and wooden bunkers were extremely vulnerable to heavy artillery fire, as the later fighting demonstrated.

It is important to note, though, that these bunkers provided a relatively safe and warm place for rest and sleep (each bunker being equipped with a stove). During the harsh winter of 1939–40 this was an extremely important aspect of everyday life for the troops.

Wooden machine-gun bunkers helped close the gaps between the concrete fortifications of the line, and could normally house one machine gun with one or two gun-ports. Army Commander of 2nd Rank Nikolai Voronov, Chief of Artillery of the Soviet 7th Army on the Karelian Isthmus, pointed out the strength of these bunkers in his post-war report to his superiors:

> The concrete, armoured and wooden bunkers on the Karelian Isthmus fitted very well into the terrain and were very well camouflaged. The strength of the fortified line was in the location of the bunkers on the reverse slopes of hills, the edges of forests and groves and behind natural obstacles. Flanking and interlocking fire of machine guns, mortars and artillery formed the basis of the Finnish system of fire. The Finnish Army is trained to fire at the enemy from the flanks in front of neighbouring units, while the Red Army, despite its high numbers of automatic weapons, is strongly inclined towards frontal fire.

Obstacles

Barbed-wire entanglements and fences were the most common infantry obstacle on the Mannerheim Line. Several variations were noted in different sectors of the Line. The Lähde and Salmenkaita sectors had barbed wire attached to spear-like steel poles, which were only 30–40cm above the ground. The overall length of the poles was about 1.5m long, so the poles were very firmly driven in. In winter, with the snow level reaching 50–100cm, these barbed-wire fences would become invisible and the Red Army infantry only became aware of them when they were already entangled. In some cases these low barbed-wire fences were combined with an anti-tank barrier made of rocks. Some fragments of these barbed-wire obstacles can still be seen today, and are especially prominent in the Lähde sector.

In other sectors barbed wire was attached to wooden poles which protruded about 60cm above the ground. There were normally four to six rows of wire at the forward obstacle line. Barbed-wire fences were also present within the defences of the Mannerheim Line itself, often forming traps for attacking infantry. The first barbed-wire fence would be built immediately in front of the flanking fire sector of a bunker, with a second fence placed behind the sector of fire. As the advancing enemy infantry negotiated the first fence, they would find themselves caught in a hail of flanking fire between the two fences. Most of the wooden poles have rotted away in time, and very little remains of these obstacles lines today.

Another variant of the barbed-wire fence saw the attachment of barbed wire directly to living trees. Such obstacles were hard to spot and were normally built between strongpoints to prevent outflanking and infiltration of the Line by Red Army scout parties. These barbed-wire fences can still be seen in the forests, as most of the trees are still growing there.

The Finnish Army was well aware of the Red Army's widespread use of armoured formations, and anti-tank obstacles were present in all sectors of the Line that featured tank-friendly terrain. The most common form of anti-tank obstacle was a barrier of granite rocks laid out in between four and twelve rows. The Finnish Army did not have sufficient funds to build these obstacles out of concrete, and the widespread presence of granite boulders and rocks in Finland made the choice of materials an obvious one. Concrete pyramids up to 2m tall saw very limited use, mostly for blocking major highways and roads.

Before the lines of rocks were emplaced, the Finnish Army conducted a series of field tests to try to resolve an obvious question about what size of rocks and how many rows would be necessary to stop an enemy tank. It was decided that four rows at a height of 70cm above the ground would render such an obstacle impassable. The rocks were buried about a metre into the ground, giving total rock height of about 1.5m. However, the problem was that the only tanks that Finland possessed in the 1930s were Renault FT-17s, dating from World War I, and Vickers six-ton tanks purchased from Great Britain. Both tanks were smaller than the Soviet T-28 medium and BT-5 light tanks. In the event, the larger Soviet tanks negotiated these obstacles with ease, which came as an extremely unpleasant surprise for the Finnish defenders.

The second serious failing of the Finnish anti-tank defences was where they were placed – namely, in front of the Mannerheim Line in open ground, where they were clearly visible from the Red Army side. This enabled the latter to employ both direct and indirect artillery fire in order to clear passages through them. In addition, the Soviet tanks themselves could clear a way through the lines by firing their main guns at the boulders; a 45mm tank cannon could destroy a rock with one direct hit.

Anti-tank ditches were employed in swampy terrain where rocks were unsuitable (they would simply sink into the bog). The sides of the ditches were strengthened with log revetments. The second line of defence in the Lähde sector was protected by an impressive anti-tank ditch, which presented a serious obstacle to Soviet armour. Once again, the weak point in the anti-tank ditches on the Mannerheim Line was their location: they were not covered by machine-gun fire, and Soviet infantry often used them as shelters from Finnish artillery fire and as a jumping-off position for an assault on the Finnish trenches.

A view of Summa village after the fighting. Soviet cars and trucks are parked in the former no-man's land. An anti-tank obstacle line is visible in the foreground. Two destroyed T-28 tanks are also visible in the centre of the picture. The Finnish bunkers are marked by vertical black lines. The picture was taken from a Soviet artillery forward observation post. (Carl-Fredrik Geust)

A modern view of the anti-tank obstacles in Lähde sector, not far from the Sj5 'Millionaire' bunker. (Bair Irincheev)

Log barriers were probably the most extravagant anti-tank obstacles on the Mannerheim Line. In wooded areas, the logs were attached horizontally to large trees, with wire at the height of a tank's turret. Hitting such an obstacle at high speed could damage a tank's gun or even remove a tank's turret. However, these barriers were given only limited use in certain areas, and are only documented in the rear of the Lähde sector.

Barricades made of fallen trees made for an obvious anti-tank obstacle in wooded terrain and were widely used on the Mannerheim Line. Such barricades were sometimes booby-trapped and combined with barbed-wire entanglements.

Another form of obstacle comprised the creation of flooded areas through the use of dams, both improvised and permanent. A tall, concrete flood dam was constructed west of the Leningrad–Viipuri railway on the Peronjoki River. When closed, the dam created a vast flooded area around the railway. A similar dam of wood and earth was built on the Majajoki River west of the Lähde sector. Once the area had been flooded and the first frosts had set in, the Finns blew up both dams. As a result, a thin layer of ice was left suspended in the air by the force of explosion, supported only by its attachment to hillocks and trees. The ice could not support the weight of even an individual soldier, rendering the terrain completely impassable for both infantry and armour.

A tree barricade in a forest, in the western part of the Karelian Isthmus. (Bair Irincheev)

Minefields were the final obstacle elements employed. Since the Finnish Army was short of money, anti-personnel minefields were almost non-existent. Most minefields were small and covered the most likely routes of armour movement. In many cases anti-tank mines were improvised devices, comprising wooden boxes filled with explosives with a

A destroyed flood dam in the Leipäsuo sector. A new forest has grown up in the intervening years, and the view does not show how tall the dam is. (Dmitry Satin)

primitive detonator attached. In the Inkilä sector the Finns used naval mines in their anti-tank minefields. The effect of such mines, each carrying 200–300kg of explosives, was devastating; a Soviet T-28 tank that drove over one of these mines before the Inkilä sector in December 1939 had its main turret blown off by the power of the explosion.

THE PRINCIPLES OF DEFENCE

The preceding description of the features of the Mannerheim Line at the outbreak of war in 1939 allows us to outline the main principles of defence. The bunkers, armed with machine guns, were only capable of stopping the enemy infantry after they had passed through the obstacle line. The sectors of fire of the bunkers were placed so that the bunkers could lay down flanking fire on the lines of barbed wire and anti-tank barrier obstacles. Bunkers often had interlocking sectors of fire. Enemy armour was supposed to be stopped by the obstacles before being dealt with by the anti-tank artillery and close-range weapons of the Finnish infantry. The Finnish officers were well aware of the weakness of their anti-tank artillery, but at the same time they knew that armour alone would not be able to control the captured terrain. Thus, the Finnish defenders of the Line saw their main task as isolating the Soviet armour from the advancing infantry and then dealing with them separately. The Finnish troops on the isthmus were issued strict orders to hold their ground and fight, even if they found themselves surrounded by the enemy.

The Finns relied on the high-quality training given to the individual Finnish infantryman, his stoicism and stubbornness, and his superior knowledge of the terrain. Each Finnish battalion that took up positions on the Mannerheim Line in October 1939 had two months to practise and prepare for all sorts of action in the terrain where the actual battles took place between December 1939 and February 1940.

Supporting artillery was stationed in fixed positions some 3–4km from the main defence line. The possible routes of advance of the Soviet troops had been carefully identified, and every metre of potential battlefield was measured and recce-ed in October and November 1939.

However, the fatal weakness in the Line was the absence of any anti-tank weaponry inside the bunkers. Apparently, in February 1940 the Finns tried to install Boys anti-tank rifles in some of the bunkers, but this proved to be of little help. Light Soviet tanks could be easily penetrated by the Boys rifle, but such rifles were scarce and few were available to each unit.

The Finnish defensive tactics on the Mannerheim Line in 1939–40 were built upon the individual stoicism and skills of the common soldier. Any strongpoint, bunker or other position was to be defended to the last man. The infantry were ordered to stay in the trenches and engage the enemy for as long as they could, even if the enemy's tanks had broken through. If a strongpoint was overrun by the enemy, it was to be regained immediately through a counterattack. Normally the Finns carried these out using sizeable platoon and company task forces, and during the hours of darkness, relying on their superior knowledge of the terrain and the trench systems. However, one major failing was that such tactics were used regardless of the situation; in some cases, a Finnish company was required to counterattack a Soviet regiment or division, with obvious catastrophic results.

THE LIVING SITES

Daily life for the Finnish defenders of the Mannerheim Line varied greatly, depending on sector of the Line and the phase of the war. The concrete shelters and bunkers (*korsu* in Finnish) were all equipped with stoves – a vital feature in the harsh winter of 1939–40. The *korsu* were seen as a safe place to be. The bunkers were lit by Petromax carbide lamps or flashlights, and, as the Finnish soldiers recalled, looked like caves from the inside.

However, the concrete bunkers built in the 1920s were obsolete by 1939 and provided only limited shelter against the heavy artillery of the Red Army, as the war diary of the 2nd Machine Gun Company, 15th Infantry Regiment of the Finnish Army during the battles in the Summankylä sector recalls: 'bunkers 5, 6 and 15 bear the brunt of the enemy's artillery fire. Our nerves are tense – the bunkers are old and cannot withstand this artillery fire for long'. The wooden dugouts and machine-gun nests, built in autumn 1939, were equally vulnerable; a single direct hit from a 6-inch shell was a death sentence to anyone inside. They became even more vulnerable when the Red Army brought up heavy 8- and 10-inch guns and mortars. Under a hurricane of artillery fire, some of the defenders would be buried alive in the ruins of collapsed bunkers, as happened in the village of Summankylä on 21 December 1939, when 19 men were killed by a direct hit on their dugout (the Kalvola Cross and Kalvola Stone now stand on the site of the destroyed dugout) and on 1 January 1940, when concrete shelter No. 4 took a direct hit, burying alive a Finnish NCO from Hattula in its ruins.

Unfinished or poorly camouflaged bunkers fell prey with similar ease to the Red Army's artillery, and could be dangerous for the defenders themselves. To make things worse, the main weapon in the Mannerheim Line bunkers was the heavy Maxim machine gun, which offered no protection against a Soviet armoured attack. With the Finnish anti-tank defences being equally weak and inadequate, Soviet armour often drove up to the bunkers, blocked the sectors of fire, and fired at the bunker's doors and gun-ports. The Finnish defenders could do little but watch helplessly.

A view from a bunker in Ilves village, in the Muolaa sector. Clearly visible are the barbed-wire obstacles and T-shaped reference marks for firing at pre-sighted targets. (Colonel Skvortsov Collection)

Different parts of the Line were subjected to artillery fire of varying intensity. The sector that was hit the worst was probably that of Summa village in the central Karelian Isthmus. The Red Army used observation balloons for orchestrating their artillery, meaning any movement in the Finnish trenches drew precise and deadly fire. As a result, any movement in the Finnish defences during daylight hours stopped. During the hours of darkness, the Finnish trenches would become 'more lively and crowded than a summer market in Joensuu', as one Finnish veteran of the battle observed.

The large bunkers built in the 1930s provided much better shelter from heavy artillery fire and would suffer significant damage only after being repeatedly hit. The 'Millionaire' bunkers, which had their living quarters about 3–4m underground, provided especially good protection. One Finnish artillery lieutenant in the Sj5 bunker recalled: 'The bunker shook like a ship in a storm during the enemy's artillery fire, but it gave a feeling of safety and protection to us. It was nice to think you were in a safe place.'

In quieter sectors life at the front was defined by routine, with troops performing regular guard duty and observing the activity of their Red Army opponents from afar.

OPERATIONAL HISTORY

The Red Army attacked all along the Soviet-Finnish border on the morning of 30 November 1939. By the end of December its ground troops had reached the Main Defence Line on the Karelian Isthmus. It is important to note that the Red Army did not advance to make contact with all sectors of the fortified line. In the central Karelian Isthmus, the Soviet advance was stopped at Lake Punnus and on the southern part of Lake Muolaa, some 10–15km south of the Line proper and its concrete bunkers. It was at this time that the name 'Mannerheim Line' was used for the first time, as a comparison with the Maginot Line in France. In the conflict that followed, each sector of the Line witnessed its own history; some sectors remained quiet and were abandoned by the Finns in an orderly fashion, some were stormed and captured by the Red Army after violent battles, whilst other sectors held out until the

A ruined early bunker in the Karhula sector, north of Karhula village. The old bunkers built in the 1920s were obsolete, and were easily spotted and destroyed by heavy Soviet artillery. (Bair Irincheev)

order came to fall back to the next lines of defence. Thus, a sector-by-sector approach to the Mannerheim Line would appear to be the most logical way of exploring this area.

The Inkilä sector

This sector remained relatively quiet all through the war, after a company of Red Army infantry supported by a platoon of T-28 tanks failed to break through along the highway between the Ink6 and Ink7 bunkers in mid-December 1939. A Finnish anti-tank gun took out two of the Soviet tanks and the third one hit a mine, which completely destroyed it. In early February 1940, both the Ink7 and Ink6 bunkers on the highway were under concentrated artillery fire of the Red Army. Ink7 took a direct hit in its front wall, with the heavy shell almost penetrating the defences, but the damage was repaired by the industrious Finns. Ink6 was subjected to a much heavier pounding, which caused its frontal armoured plates to crack. Damage was also done to the armoured roofs of the bunkers, which Finnish pioneers had to strengthen with two layers of concrete blocks.

The Russian seaman Mikhail M. Garmoza, the gun-layer of a 6-inch gun, fired at the two bunkers over open sights, ignoring the machine-gun and rifle fire of the Finnish defenders. For his bravery he was awarded the top military

C — THE INK6 BUNKER, IN THE INKILÄ SECTOR, EARLY FEBRUARY 1940

The bunker was bombarded by both direct and indirect fire from the Soviet heavy artillery. The two layers of rocks on top of the casemates are field repairs given to the bunker by Finnish sappers.

Despite heavy bombardment, the bunker remained operational and acted in the defence of the Line until the evening of 15 February 1940, when the withdrawal from the Mannerheim Line began.

The Ink6 bunker, in the Inkilä sector, early February 1940

RIGHT
Soviet light T-26 tanks from the 35th Light Tank Brigade on the Karelian Isthmus. The T-26, derived from the British Vickers 6-ton tank, was a primary weapon of the Soviet light tank brigades on the isthmus, along with BT tanks. Note the rough snow camouflage and an early model T-26 tank with two machine-gun turrets on the right. The 35th Light Tank Brigade supported the Red Army infantry units in Summa village and the Lähde sectors. (Carl-Fredrik Geust)

decoration of the USSR, the Gold Star of Hero of the Soviet Union (medal No. 457). His gun belonged to a battery supporting the actions of the naval infantry of the Baltic Fleet in the Inkilä sector. Despite the damage and continuous assaults both by naval infantry over the frozen Gulf of Finland and on land by the infantry of the 42nd Rifle Division, the Finns firmly held on.

As the Finnish Army withdrew from the Mannerheim Line on 15 February 1940, the bunkers of the Inkilä sector were captured by the Red Army intact. Before being blown up, they were used in two cinema productions: a Soviet propaganda film entitled 'Mannerheim Line' (1940), and 'Frontline Girlfriends' (1940).

BELOW
The armoured casemates of the Ink6 bunker. The two layers of rocks are the work of field repair of the bunker after a Soviet bombardment. Even with two additional layers of rocks on the roof, the bunker is only barely visible in the terrain. The devastating effect of Soviet artillery fire is obvious in this photo. (Carl-Fredrik Geust)

Karhula

The Karhula sector featured several concrete bunkers on the hill north of the eponymous village, but the Red Army's advance was stopped a couple of kilometres to the south, at Marjapellonmäki hill. Despite strong attacks that

often resulted in hand-to-hand fighting in the trenches on the hill, the Finnish lines held in December and January, and only began to crumble during the Soviet offensive in February 1940.

Summa village (Summankylä)

At the outbreak of the Winter War the Summa village sector, located on one of the three main highways to Vyborg, was one of the strongest of the whole Main Defence Line. The sector featured anti-tank obstacles stretching from the Summajoki River to Lake Summajärvi, a barbed-wire fence around platoon strongpoints and a vast network of trenches. The fortifications of the Line were right in the middle of Summa village, which had over 50 houses, a school and a village shop before the war.

The sector had a total of 17 concrete bunkers, with three bunkers of the 'Millionaire' type (Sk2 'Terttu', Sk11 'Peltola' and Sk10 'The Ten'). The other bunkers were weaker ones, dating back to the 1920s. Small minefields were built in front of Sk2 'Terttu', on the highway, and south from Sk10 'The Ten' bunker. Defending the sector was the 2nd Battalion, 15th Infantry Regiment from Häme province in Finland, under Captain Jensson. In October and November 1939, before war broke out, the Finnish battalion built more fortifications, cleared sectors of fire for the bunkers and carried out refreshment training for personnel of the battalion, a large part of which had been drafted from reserve. Most of the civilians of Summa village had been evacuated, with a few teenage boys left behind to take care of the village cattle. These teenage boys also assisted the men of the 15th Infantry Regiment in the construction of the defences.

On 6 December 1939, as the frontline drew closer to Summa village, Captain Jensson's men set fire to the village, a scene witnessed by the teenage boys, who were packing up to leave. This was a common practice of the Finnish Army in the Winter War. The invader was to be deprived of any warmth or shelter in the harsh Finnish winter conditions.

The attacking Red Army units (138th Rifle Division, 35th Light Tank Brigade and 20th Heavy Tank Brigade) made contact with the Finnish Main

A close-up view of the Ink6 casemate. Note the crack on the frontal armoured plate, missing bolts, traces of direct hits and evidence of field repair. Two observation slits and a gun-port are clearly visible. The gun-port provided only a very narrow sector of fire, of about 60 degrees. (Carl-Fredrik Geust)

The Summa village (Summankylä) sector of the Mannerheim Line

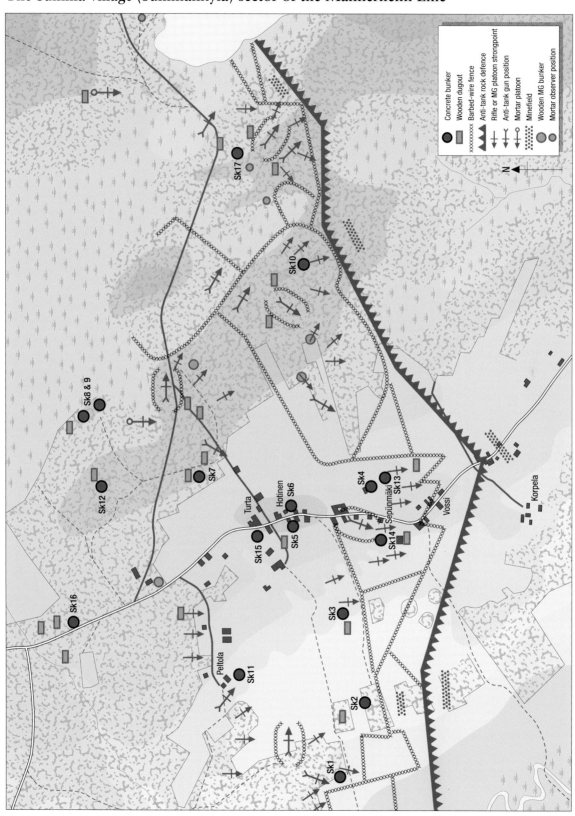

Legend:
- Concrete bunker
- Wooden dugout
- Barbed-wire fence
- Anti-tank rock defence
- Rifle or MG platoon strongpoint
- Anti-tank gun position
- Mortar platoon
- Minefield
- Wooden MG bunker
- Mortar observer position

Labels: Sk17, Sk10, Sk8 & 9, Sk7, Sk12, Sk4, Sk13, Sepünmäki, Sk14, Vossi, Korpela, Turta, Hotinen, Sk6, Sk5, Sk15, Sk16, Sk3, Peltola, Sk11, Sk2, Sk1

A direct hit on the wall of the
Ink7 bunker, which almost
penetrated the bunker's shell.
Note the H-shaped metal bars
used by Finnish engineers
to repair the damage.
(Bair Irincheev)

The entrance to the Sk10
'The Ten' bunker. Like the
Ink6 bunker, the Sk10 had
casemates with an armoured
roof and a frontal wall.
(Bair Irincheev)

Defence Line on 12–13 December 1939. After a few probing assaults, the first Soviet offensive against the Line took place between 17 and 19 December, with a culmination push on 19 December. On that day the 138th Rifle Division hit the Finnish defenders with two regiments of infantry supported by about 80 light, medium and heavy tanks.

Although the Soviet commanders were aware of the presence of the Finnish fortified line, the precise location of the Finnish bunkers was not known to them. The only elements of the Finnish defence that scouts of the 138th Rifle Division managed to spot were anti-tank obstacles and the barbed-wire fences.

During the three days of the battle the Soviet armour (105th Light Tank Battalion, 90th Heavy Tank Battalion and the Independent Heavy Tank Company) negotiated the Finnish obstacle line, broke through the Finnish defences and drove towards Viipuri. The Finnish anti-tank guns were destroyed in an uneven fight with the two Soviet tank battalions. However, the infantry regiments of the 138th Rifles were stopped by concentrated machine-gun fire from the Finnish bunkers and trenches. During darkness, which in December sets in already at 16.00, Finnish tank destroyers managed to damage or destroy most of the Soviet tanks that remained behind their defence line in the forest north of Summa village.

As a result, having lost about 25 tanks, the Red Army made no further progress in the sector. The losses suffered by the 138th Rifles remain unclear but the divisional staff itself described them as 'heavy'. The Finnish 2nd Battalion of the 15th Infantry Regiment that defended the sector suffered relatively light casualties, which can be estimated at about 30–50 men killed in action. The gun company of the regiment had suffered extremely heavy losses – all its guns and 11 men killed, including the company commander. (In December 1939 the official name of the anti-tank gun battery of the 15th Infantry Regiment labelled it a 'gun company').

On 21 December 1939, Kirill Meretskov, Commander of the North-Western Front, sent a message to Moscow stating that the Red Army units had come across a formidable fortified line and more resources were necessary to deal with it. Large-scale operations on the isthmus were halted. During the rest of December 1939 and January 1940 the Red Army artillery delivered systematic strikes against the Finnish defences in the Summa village sector and carefully prepared for a new offensive scheduled for early February 1940. The Soviet artillery employed observation balloons to coordinate its fire. One by one the Finnish bunkers were picked out and destroyed or badly damaged by Soviet artillery. Throughout December 1939 and January 1940 the Red Army continued to bring more heavy artillery pieces into position all the time.

In early January 1940 both the Finns and Soviets rotated their troops at the front in the Summa village sector; the Finns brought in the fresh 7th Infantry Regiment, while the Red Army brought in the 100th Rifle Division from Byelorussia. Unlike the first wave of Soviet rifle divisions, which marched into Finland in light autumn uniforms, the 100th Rifles were fully equipped with the best winter uniforms the Red Army had.

In the meantime, the Soviet artillery continued to rain heavy shells down on Summa village. On 21 December 1939 a heavy Soviet grenade hit a dugout of the 5th Company, 15th Infantry Regiment at Summa village, burying all 19 soldiers alive inside. On 25 December 1939, the Sk5 bunker was hit and its older part was completely destroyed. The Sk11 Peltola bunker was hit on 27 December; two heavy rounds penetrated the roof of the accommodation chambers, killing two soldiers and destroying the central heating system of the bunker. As a result, the accommodation chambers were filled with water and became unfit for use. The Sk15 shelter was hit several times, but was still in use by the Finns. The Sk14 shelter became flooded after heavy shells fell on the surrounding terrain and changed the flow of the ground water. The Sk4 shelter was hit in late December and finally collapsed on 1 January 1940, burying Finnish Sergeant Ernest Daniel Pohjola inside. The Sk7 shelter, used as an ammunition store, was hit and collapsed on 15 January 1940. The Sk3 bunker was blown up during the night of 13–14 January by a scout party from the 355th Rifle Regiment, 100th Rifle Division. Senior Lieutenant Vatagin and Sergeant Kirillov were awarded the Gold Star for their part in this action. The Sk2 'Terttu' bunker was damaged by a heavy artillery barrage in late January 1940. The Sk5 bunker had its armoured tower blown into pieces by direct fire from a Soviet 45mm anti-tank cannon. The crew of the cannon from the 330th Rifle Regiment fired over 200 armour-piercing rounds at the tower and thus managed to penetrate the thick armour of the turret. The Sk6 bunker was hit several times, but was still in a relatively good condition. The bunkers to the east of the highway, Sk10 'The Ten' and Sk17 'Iines', were left alone for the time being.

As a result of a month-long artillery barrage, by the beginning of the next Soviet offensive on 1 February 1940 most of the Finnish concrete bunkers were either damaged or had been reduced to heaps of rubble. The 4th Rifle Company, 355th Rifle Regiment began a carefully planned reconnaissance in force on 1 February 1940. The company, supported by three medium T-28 tanks and a sapper platoon, managed to capture and hold the Sk1 and Sk2 bunkers after a series of heavy hand-to-hand engagements that took place between 1 and 3 February 1940, but the Finns managed to contain all the assaults that followed. The Sk2 and Sk1 bunkers were destroyed with explosives on 3–4 February 1940. Red Army sappers claimed to have used 5,300kg of explosives to destroy the Sk2 'Terttu' bunker.

All the attempts by the 100th Rifle Division to repeat the success of the scout party on 13 January, when the Sk3 bunker was blown up, failed. Assault parties of riflemen, armour and sappers with explosives were sent forward on numerous occasions. They were all stopped by machine-gun fire and failed to reach the Finnish bunkers. Nevertheless, the units of the 100th Rifle Division attacked the Finnish defences in Summa village every day, with little or no result. The shattered line of Finnish defences managed to hang by a thread. The Finnish infantry was exhausted by the constant fighting, but held out until the retreat order came on 15 February 1940. During the retreat the Finns burnt down or blew up the remaining bunkers and dugouts.

Lähde

The Lähde sector of defence stretched from Lake Summajärvi in the west to the Munasuo swamp in the east. The Finnish defences were anchored on the two formidable bunkers built in the area in the second half of the 1930s: the Sj5 'Miljoonalinnake' ('Millionaire fort') on Tongue hill and the Sj4 'Poppiuslinnake' ('Fort of Poppius') at the road to Kämärä station. The rest of the fortifications in the sector dated back to the 1920s; except for the strong Sj6 'Torsu' command bunker, in 1939 they had limited defensive value. The defenders of this crucial sector were the men of the 1st Battalion, 15th Infantry Regiment under the energetic and experienced Jäger Captain Auno Kuiri.

The 123rd Rifle Division of Colonel Stenshinski appeared before the Finnish defences in mid-December 1939. The offensive started on the 17th with the

A unique feature of the Sk10 'The Ten' bunker was the elevator for the heavy machine gun. The gun was hidden inside the bunker during enemy artillery action and only lifted into firing position during the actual assault. The mount was experimental and was only used in the Sk10. (Bair Irincheev)

The remains of the armoured wall of one of the eastern casemates of Sk10 'The Ten'. An empty 6-inch shell lies next to the armoured debris. Soon after the photo was taken, the debris was looted for scrap metal. (Bair Irincheev)

support of tanks from the 91st Heavy Tank Battalion and the 101st Light Tank Battalion. The 245th Rifle Regiment attacked on the left flank in the area of the Sj5 bunker, and the 255th Rifle Regiment attacked in the middle of the sector. Together with common armour, the attack was supported by two flamethrower tanks, which attacked the trenches at the Harkkila strongpoint.

D A FINNISH WOODEN MACHINE-GUN BUNKER, IN THE LÄHDE SECTOR

Although Finnish pre-war fortification manuals had provided drawings for how bunkers of all types should be built, the Finns often constructed the bunkers according to the locally available materials, the terrain features encountered, the presence or proximity of ground water, and common sense. These wooden bunkers, along with trench works, were the backbone of the Finnish defences in many sectors that lacked concrete bunkers. The bunkers featured two Maxim heavy machine guns, and provided protection against light field guns and Soviet tanks, but were easily destroyed by heavy 6-inch guns when spotted.

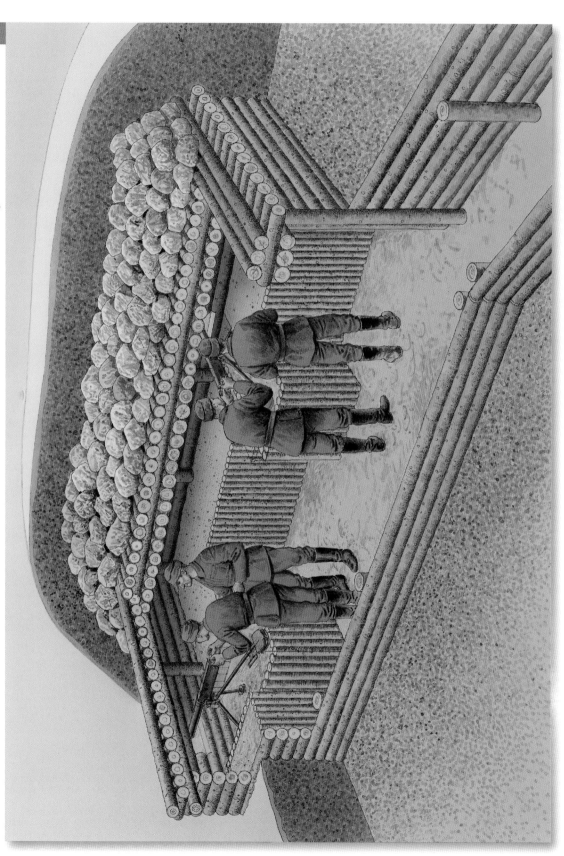

A Finnish wooden machine-gun bunker, in the Lähde sector

A Soviet B-4 8-inch gun in position on the Karelian Isthmus. A unique feature of the battles on the Mannerheim Line was the deployment of these formidable guns for firing over open sights at a distance of only 700–1,500m from the Finnish bunkers. This demanded careful and secret preparation of a firing position, camouflage, and nerves of steel among the gun crew, who would have to fire at the Finnish fortifications whilst under the rain of mortar fire that the Finns would quickly bring down on these weapons. Red Army soldiers dubbed these weapons 'Karelian sculptors' while the Finns called them 'Stalin's sledgehammers'. (Carl-Fredrik Geust)

Two Finnish platoon leaders, 2nd Lieutenants Harkkila and Louhi, were killed in the middle of the defence sector early on during the Soviet assault. This greatly reduced the battle effectiveness of the Finnish infantry, and the Red Army achieved two limited breakthroughs in the Finnish defences. They besieged the central bunker of the sector, Sj4 'Poppius', and captured about 70m of trenches at the Harkkila strongpoint. Over 100 Finns retreated into the besieged bunker: infantry, signals operators, tank-destroyer teams, artillery observers, machine gunners. The bunker was designed to accommodate only 40 men, and the air started to run out in the bunker during the night of 17–18 December.

Soviet armour broke through the defences and drove into the Finnish rear, blocking the exits from dugouts and causing confusion. When Captain Auno Kuiri heard about the breakthrough at the frontline, he left the command bunker in order to inspect the situation in person. After walking 50m towards the 'Poppius' bunker, he was pinned down by machine-gun fire from five advancing Soviet tanks. Kuiri had to hide in a shell crater all day long, and a rumour spread around the battalion that he had been killed. Several Soviet tanks surrounded the command bunker of the battalion. The battalion staff officers burnt all the papers and prepared for the worse. However, despite this critical situation, the infantry of the 255th Rifle Regiment advanced no further than the trenches around the 'Poppius' bunker. The Soviet tanks in the Finnish rear blew their horns and fired signal flares, urging their infantry escort to follow, but with no result. This gave the Finns time to regroup and restore the chain of command. As darkness set in, Soviet tanks in the Finnish rear started their drive back to the jumping-off positions, fearing Finnish infantry assaults during the night. During the whole day of 17 December 1939, two machine guns from the eastern casemate of the 'Millionaire' bunker fired without respite, shooting an estimated 40,000 rounds at the advancing infantry of the 245th and 255th Rifles.

Although two battalions of the 255th Rifles, with the support of three immobilized tanks, held the 'Poppius' bunker under siege and occupied the trenches around it, all further attacks by the Red Army were contained. The Finns managed to push the infantry of the 245th Rifles from Harkkila strongpoint in the evening of 17 December. Two battalions of the 255th Rifles held out for six more days. On 21 December 1939 the Soviet tanks fired at the eastern casemate of the 'Poppius' bunker at point-blank range using their main guns, causing substantial damage to the bunker's gun-ports. On the same day a Soviet assault party blew up the eastern entrance to the bunker, but the damage was insignificant and the Finns quickly made it good using sandbags. The 255th Rifles could not advance any further. Their officer losses were too high; the regiment had lost all three battalion commanders and two battalion chiefs of staff killed and wounded by 22 December.

The Finns finally managed to liquidate the breakthrough on the night of 22–23 December 1939. Only the third of three Finnish attacks succeeded after a series of fierce hand-to-hand fighting in the trenches around 'Poppius'. The rest of December 1939 and January 1940 was filled with small skirmishes and scout party raids from both sides. The 123rd Rifle Division dug in and started preparing for the offensive, while the Finns rotated the troops (the 1st Battalion, 15th Infantry Regiment was replaced by the 2nd Battalion, 8th Infantry Regiment under Captain Oksanen). Colonel Stenshinski, commander of the 123rd Rifle Division, was replaced by Colonel Alyabushev.

On 27–28 January 1940 Soviet heavy 6-inch guns, placed in firing positions over open sights, inflicted serious damage on both the key bunkers in the area – Sj4 'Poppius' and Sj5 'Millionaire'. The former had one of its armoured casemates

ABOVE
A Soviet artilleryman poses with a shell from his gun. 'The effect of the enemy's direct artillery fire was great, especially on the morale of our troops', noted a Finnish lieutenant in the Salmenkaita sector. (Carl-Fredrik Geust)

LEFT
The effect of a Soviet artillery barrage on a forest. A Finnish officer in the Karhula sector described the battlefield there in February as a good illustration of what Dante's Inferno would look like. (Carl-Fredrik Geust)

heavily damaged and a section of the underground accommodation chamber collapsed. Two soldiers were killed inside. Sj5 'Millionaire' had two of its three armoured towers shot off by direct hits, with an artillery observer killed in the eastern tower. One of the eastern casemates was completely destroyed and the second eastern casemate was heavily damaged. Lieutenant Akim G. Grachev, Fire Section Leader, 24th Corps Artillery Regiment, who personally directed the fire of the heavy cannons, was awarded the Gold Star of the Hero of the Soviet Union for this achievement (Medal No. 194).

The Finns again rotated their troops on 10 February 1940, just one day before the main Soviet offensive. The weakened 2nd Battalion, 9th Infantry Regiment, replaced the battalion of Captain Oksanen at the frontline. To make things worse, the battalion was formed from Swedish-speaking Finnish soldiers. This meant that there was no common language between different Finnish units in the area.

The Soviet artillery preparation in the sector on 11 February 1940 was one of the largest ever, smaller only than the artillery barrage that was laid down at the battle of Verdun. This came as a shock to the Finnish defenders who had only been stationed in quiet sectors of the Mannerheim Line before. The assaulting Soviet parties quickly captured the ruins of the Sj4 'Poppius' bunker. The company of Lieutenant Malm, which was defending the centre of the Lähde sector at 'Poppius', lost over 80 per cent of its men in one day on 11 February 1940. Soviet armour and infantry continued from 'Poppius' to the Test bunker and the Sj6 'Torsu' command bunker. Soviet troops surrounded the latter and demanded its surrender, threatening to blow up the bunker with all 29 men inside. As the bunker was full of the wounded, the Finnish medics made the decision to surrender it in order to save the lives of the men.

On the right flank of the sector the 'Millionaire' bunker held out until 13 February. The Soviet infantry pushed the Finnish defenders from the trenches south of the bunker and made it to the roof of the western casemate, closer to the lake. They threw rocks and stones down from the roof, blocking the door.

Soviet T-28 heavy tanks from the 20th Heavy Tank Brigade preparing for an attack, in February 1940. These tanks were the main heavy tank type on the Karelian Isthmus during the battles on the Mannerheim Line. The battalions and companies of the 20th Heavy Tank Brigade supported Red Army infantry units in the Summa village, Lähde, Taasionlammet and Inkilä sectors of the Mannerheim Line. (Carl-Fredrik Geust)

The Finns counterattacked from the eastern casemate, forcing the Soviet infantry to retreat. An anti-tank team manning a 37mm Bofors cannon and artillery observers left the bunker soon afterwards. Lieutenant Ericsson, commander of the 5th Company, left the bunker as well, ordering the platoon under 2nd Lieutenant Skade to hold the bunker at any cost. The morale of the defenders deteriorated after the departure of their company commander. The soldiers saw that the bunker might well become their common grave and sought any excuse to leave the bunker and withdraw to the second line of the defences. As a result, only six men were inside the bunker on 12 February when the order to withdraw finally came through to the bunker, brought by two runners. Rafael Forth, one of the six men, followed the order and left the bunker with the runners, but was taken prisoner by the advancing Red Army. The remaining men decided to stay in the bunker a bit longer. Finally, the last defenders were surrounded in the bunker by Soviet infantry and sappers. After they refused to surrender, the bunker was blown up and all the men, except for Private Gunnar Storm, were killed. Storm was wounded and taken prisoner. Small units from the 8th Infantry Regiment tried to counterattack and recapture the bunker, but failed under the heavy fire of machine guns on the Soviet side.

The Finns counterattacked with several fresh battalions on 12 and 13 February, but these failed. After a day of fighting, units of the 123rd Rifle Division supported by armour crossed the anti-tank ditch at the second line of Finnish defences and continued their thrust forward. The Finns had lost all their anti-tank guns on the Mannerheim Line and had no more long-range anti-tank weapons left. Temperatures on 13–14 February descended to -30 degrees Celsius, making operations in the open extremely difficult. Some of the exhausted Finnish soldiers were falling asleep and freezing to death in their hastily dug snow trenches. Communications were breaking down and the Finns could no longer call for artillery strikes on the advancing Soviet troops. The breakdown doomed

A modern-day view of Summa village. The small hillocks to the left of the road are the ruins of bunkers Sk15 and Sk5, while the larger hillock to the right is the destroyed bunker Sk6. (Bair Irincheev)

Red Army soldiers study the western, less damaged casemate of the Sj4 'Poppius' bunker in March 1940. Barely visible in the background are the remains of two destroyed medium T-28 tanks.
(Bair Irincheev)

the men of the 2nd Heavy Artillery Battalion. The Finnish infantry failed to inform this battalion about the Soviet breakthrough and it was taken completely by surprise when Soviet armour stormed their positions from the rear. Eleven howitzers were captured by the tanks of Captain Arkhipov. Thirty-two artillerymen locked themselves in a dugout, while the rest fled their positions into the nearby forests. As the Finns inside the dugout refused to surrender, the Soviet sappers blew the dugout up with all the defenders inside. This dugout was later dubbed 'the Death bunker'.

Despite Finnish counterattacks, the Soviet breakthrough grew to such an extent that the whole Mannerheim Line had to be abandoned on 15 February 1940. The breakthrough and the repelling of Finnish counterattacks came at a high cost to the 123rd Rifle Division, especially in terms of its commanders. Captain Soroka, a battalion commander in the 245th Regiment, and Senior Lieutenant Yemelyanov, who was personally leading his company against the 'Millionaire' bunker, were killed in action. Both were posthumously awarded with the Gold Star of the Hero of the Soviet Union.

Leipäsuo

The defences of this sector comprised two armoured bunkers covering the Leningrad–Vyborg railway line, five old bunkers about two kilometres north also on the frontline, and a flood dam on the Peronjoki River.

In December 1939 the Finns held their lines with ease, but in February the Red Army placed several heavy pieces in firing positions over open sights and heavily damaged both bunkers No. 6 and No. 7. Captain Fedenko described the battle in his memoirs:

> The barbed-wire obstacles ran along the Peronjoki River on the front, some seven metres wide. The Finns dammed the river up and it flooded an area some 500m wide and froze. After the ice had become some 20cm thick, the dam was destroyed; water ran from the flooded area under the ice, and the ice was left hanging on the small islands and hillocks some three metres above the water. The hanging ice was covered by one metre of snow. People could walk on it, but it would not hold the weight of tanks.
>
> On our side of the river we discovered minefields under the ice, and swampy areas that remained unfrozen some three kilometres wide. The railway bridge

was blown up and opposite it there was a group of bunkers, which were protected, as we found out later, by walls of seven steel plates, each 48mm thick, bolted together.

The entire area in front of the bunkers was under machine-gun, cannon and mortar fire from the bunkers.

We had to break through the defensive line and destroy the enemy...

Opposite the Finnish bunker No. 239 on our bank of the river there was a small elevation covered by trees. The engineer platoon leader Shikov proposed cutting a path through the forest and putting the bunker under direct fire. The elevation was protected from the flanking machine-gun fire of the other bunkers by the remains of the railway embankment.

The commanders approved Shikov's plan.

The next morning I was already lying in a snow trench on the rise opposite the bunker. Shikov and his engineers cut the path through the forest during the night.

Artillery men rolled the gun into position and aimed it at the fortification. Finnish bullets started hitting the armoured shield of the gun like peas from a peashooter, and hissed above our heads. The snow started moving and hissing from long machine-gun bursts from the bunker. The gun fired its first shot. The shell exploded about 100 meters from us. We saw a long tongue of flame shooting into the sky, and splinters flew in our direction. The gun fired 25 shells, but each time we could only see long red flames around the bunker. It was invincible – the shells ricocheted off the sloping armoured wall.

The Finns opened mortar fire on us. The rounds hissed through the air, exploding next to us, showering us with snow. Four artillery men had already been wounded. The gun was pulled back from the position. Shikov ran up to me, his face red and covered with sweat.

'It's OK. We will get them anyway!' he shouted.

Using tree trunks for cover we started to examine the bunker. Through our binoculars we could spot slight damage at the point where the armour connected with the concrete. The artillery officer ordered us to employ anti-concrete shells ... As soon as we had received concrete-busting shells, we rolled the 152mm gun into position opposite Bunker 239. The wide barrel of the gun was aimed

The destroyed eastern casemate of the Sj5 'Millionaire' bunker. Note the remains of the camouflage net in the upper right corner of the picture. (Carl-Fredrik Geust)

point-blank at the small dark spot at the bunker's base. Thus we started the 'chiselling' of the bunker. With support from the divisional artillery, which was suppressing the mortars and distracting the attention of the Finnish artillery bunkers, we opened fire on the spot where the concrete connected with steel. The gun was firing at one spot. Flames were shooting into the air, which shuddered with each blast of the gun. I was observing the explosions from a shelter. I wanted to see the end of the bunker, but it resisted still.

Wounded artillery men were replaced again and again on the gun, but the firing did not stop. Finally, we saw smoke emerging from the gun-ports of the bunker.

'Fire!', repeated the gun commander again and again, and several other shells hit the gaping hole. The mass of concrete and steel was silenced for good. I saw the artillery men smiling. Suddenly the neighbouring bunker No. 167 also became silent, although there were no signs of destruction on it. After some time our infantry consolidated its position in the silenced bunkers.

When I visited the destroyed fortifications later, I saw the fearsome power of our weaponry. The 1.5m-thick concrete ceiling had collapsed together with the 7m of soil on top of it. The steel walls were bent and in the neighbouring bunker No. 167 the plates around the gun-port had closed up. Now it was clear why this bunker had also become silent.

The Finnish defenders held out until 15 February, though, when the withdrawal order was given.

Taasionlammet

The Finns did not have any concrete fortifications in this area and the defensive works comprised field fortifications: trenches, wooden dugouts, barbed-wire obstacles, wooden machine-gun bunkers, an anti-tank ditch at the Suursuo swamp and a few minefields. During December 1939 Red Army units failed to achieve any success in the area, suffering light casualties from the 14th Infantry Regiment that was defending the sector. The commander of the 24th Rifle Division, Kombrig Veshev, was killed in a skirmish with Finnish troops on 6 December 1939. During the rest of December and January 1940 the 24th Division spent time carefully rehearsing the offensive and reducing the Finnish fortifications.

The new Soviet offensive across the Suursuo swamp started on 11 February 1940. After a massive artillery preparation three rifle battalions of the 24th Rifle Division slowly pushed forward across the swamp on skis with the support of light tanks, taking cover behind armoured shields (dubbed 'LBT' by the Red Army infantry). The advancing Soviet infantry captured a section of the Finnish trenches in the K3 strongpoint defended by a platoon of 2nd Lieutenant Savinen, of 9th Company, 2nd Infantry Brigade. Finnish counterattacks led to nothing, but, after receiving reinforcements, the Finns managed to contain any further advance of the 24th Rifle Division. On 12 February the offensive continued. Soviet tanks managed to reach the shallow trenches of strongpoint L1 and forced the Finnish infantry to abandon the strongpoint, firing their main uns and machine guns along the trenches. The commander of the Finnish 2nd Brigade sent a reinforced infantry company with one 37mm anti-tank gun to deal with the crisis, and the Soviet advance was again stopped. However, the reinforced company was immediately engaged by superior forces of Soviet infantry and could no longer be withdrawn from the frontline. This left the brigade in a dangerous situation without any reserves to hand.

The Sj3 bunker showing field repairs completed by Finnish sappers; sandbags were added to the damaged parts of the bunker. The Red Army artillery pounded the Finnish defences during the daytime, and Finnish sappers repaired them every night in the bitter cold. (Carl-Fredrik Geust)

The anti-tank gun could not be transported to the frontline due to the difficult terrain and had to be returned to the brigade HQ. Hand-to-hand fight continued in the trenches all day, and neither side could gain the upper hand over the other. The situation was unclear in the confusion of the fighting and neither side could report exact losses, as fallen Red Army men and Finns were lying in the trenches in five layers on top of each other.

On 13 February the attacking infantry of the 24th Rifles managed to reach the dugout area of the K3 strongpoint, but was thrown back by a fresh company under Lieutenant Zilliacus, which arrived there at the last moment. The Finns received a 13mm Boys anti-tank rifle in the afternoon and managed to damage several Soviet light tanks, but other tanks made it across the swamp. Soviet sappers built their own machine-gun bunker at K3 and frustrated any Finnish attempts at movement in the open. During the night of 13–14 February the temperature descended to a bitingly cold –30 degrees Celsius, which made operations even harder for both sides.

The Finns managed to contain the Soviet attacks on 14 February and decided to reduce the Soviet-built bunker. However, due to the extreme cold most of the mortar rounds that were fired at the Soviet bunker did not explode and Finnish forces earmarked for the attack were insufficient. On 14 February there were only 248 men left in the forward battalions of the Finnish brigade defending a three-kilometre-wide front.

In the morning of 15 February the Soviet assault continued and Soviet riflemen again reached the dugout area. Finnish resources were all but spent. After receiving a desperate request for help from the remains of the 9th Company that was defending the K3 strongpoint, the HQ of the brigade could only send 25 drivers and support staff from the 2nd Battalion – all the support staff of the 3rd Battalion had long been fighting at the frontline already. When the order to withdraw came in the afternoon, the reserves of the 2nd Brigade were all spent and the Finnish defenders were hanging on by a thread. However, the Finns managed to successfully disengage and withdraw to the intermediary line, after leaving several delaying parties in the way of the advancing 24th Rifles.

The key role in defending the whole sector was executed by the exemplary, brave, single infantry platoon under 2nd Lieutenant Savinen defending the

The Sj3 bunker after demolition by Red Army sappers. Note the H-shaped bars, typical reinforcements for the roofs of bunkers in the 1920s. (Carl-Fredrik Geust)

K3 strongpoint. During four days of constant fighting his platoon shrank from 32 men on 10 February to just 11 men on the 15th.

The ferocity of the battles in the Taasionlammet sector was repeated in the Merkki sector of the Mannerheim Line west of the Leningrad–Viipuri railway. Similar actions with small breakthroughs by the Red Army were also fought in the Merkki area around the Leningrad–Viipuri railway and around the Munasuo swamp at the eastern flank of the Lähde sector. Although the Red Army managed limited penetrations of the Finnish defences, the Finns managed to contain the Soviet advance until the order came to withdraw to the next line of defences – although this came at a high cost of expending their precious reserves.

Suurniemi

This sector had five new machine-gun bunkers and two new concrete shelters by the time war broke out. The Soviet attacks were concentrated on the

Traces of direct hits from the main guns of tanks, anti-tank guns and heavy artillery mark the frontal wall of the eastern casemate of the Sj4 'Poppius' bunker. Soviet artillery Sergeant Egorov was awarded a Gold Star of Hero of the Soviet Union for firing at the casemate at almost point-blank range, after all his fellow crew members were killed or wounded. (Carl-Fredrik Geust)

Taasionlammet sector, but the Suurniemi bunkers came under heavy artillery fire from the Soviet side during the whole assault against the Mannerheim Line. Bunkers nos. 1 and 5 were especially badly damaged. The industrious Soviet artillery crews built wooden bunkers for heavy cannons on the Suursuo swamp at night and would only roll a heavy cannon into position during daytime. The Finns destroyed the bunkers when withdrawing from the sector during the night of 15–16 February 1940.

Muolaa

The Muolaa sector is different to other parts of the Line; its modernization in the 1930s was an attempt to create a well-echeloned defensive line. The bunkers dating from the 1920s were located on steep ridges at Kangaspelto village and north of a small stream that flows from Lake Muolaanlampi into Lake Muolaanjärvi. The first line of defences had several machine-gun bunkers for frontal fire and also boasted a bunker with a 75mm Meller cannon that had a superb field of fire westwards to the Kivenappa–Viipuri highway. The cannon could fire into the right flank of advancing Soviet troops. Thus, already in the 1920s the sector had two lines of defence with a depth of about 1.5km. The new bunkers were built even further to the rear, in some 1.5km from the stream. As of February 1940, the fortified line had three lines of anti-tank obstacles, several barbed-wire fences and three lines of concrete bunker defence.

The last and newest line of bunkers was not ready when war broke out, which proved fatal for some of the defenders of the Mannerheim Line in this sector. The trench works were incomplete, communication lines were often missing and, worst of all, the new bunkers were uncamouflaged. The concrete accommodation bunkers were missing altogether – when hostilities started, only the floors of the shelters had been put in place. As one Finnish veteran of the battle put it: 'In the grey forest the black bunkers could be seen standing from miles away. They were such rat holes that I still wonder how the enemy did not cremate us all inside those bunkers.'

Heavy fighting lasted for about ten days in the area, from 17–27 February 1940. The Red Army units captured the first, old line of bunkers in a matter of

The armoured tower of a Finnish bunker destroyed by a direct hit from a heavy Soviet shell. (Carl-Fredrik Geust)

The Mu19 bunker, in the Muolaa sector, mid-February 1940

two days. The Finns did not have any intention of stopping the advancing Red Army at the old line, and instead prepared for the main battle on the modern bunker line. However, a dramatic one-day battle for bunker No. 1 took place on 21 February 1940. The Soviet probing infantry attack started at 08.00 after a massive artillery barrage, but it was repelled. Then the commanders of the Soviet 136th Rifle Division called in the heavy artillery of the 137th Heavy Artillery Regiment to pinpoint and destroy the bunker. Captain Shevenok, a battery commander in the 137th, reflected on his orders for the battle:

> 'Right here,' the Chief of Artillery said, 'somewhere in this corner, between the lake and the river, there is a bunker. Well, it is your job to find its exact location. The infantry tried to advance on the ice of the lake and the stream, but all came to nothing. It looks like they have up to 10 machine guns in an area of 300 by 400 metres. We must knock that bunker out at any cost … The infantry said they saw its gun-ports on the left as they attacked.'

A modern view of field repairs on a destroyed armoured tower on the central part of the Sj5 'Millionaire' bunker. The remains of the armoured tower were removed, a hole in the roof was filled with concrete and a pipe for a periscope was added. Note the direct hits from bullets on the pipe, a witness to the ferocity of the fighting around the bunker. (Bair Irincheev)

E **THE MU19 BUNKER, IN THE MUOLAA SECTOR, MID-FEBRUARY 1940**

The bunker was built in the summer and autumn of 1939, just before the outbreak of the Winter War, and represented the latest fortification design. It was armed with two heavy Maxim machine guns set up for flanking fire, and also had numerous gun-ports for light machine guns and rifles. When the battles in the Muolaa sector began on 21 February 1940, the new bunkers like this one had not yet been properly camouflaged, which proved fatal for some of the Finnish defenders. In addition to poor camouflage, these bunkers lacked anti-tank weapons. In battle they were destroyed by Soviet armoured units, which employed some 30 flamethrower vehicles during the battle of Muolaa.

Captain Shevenok set up his forward observation post a mere 150m from the bunker and called in the artillery power of his mighty 203mm guns:

> After about 15–20 shots one of our rounds hit the bunker, ricocheted off and exploded off-target, but nevertheless cut down one of the pine trees on top of the bunker. Several minutes later the next round tore off the protective layer of stones from the roof of the bunker. Our infantry tried to advance on the right, but was pinned down. The bunker opened fire. And finally, we scored a direct hit on the armoured cupola of the bunker. I saw the Finns fleeing the bunker.

Although the Finnish infantry retreated from the trenches and the bunker, machine-gun crews, an artillery observer team under Lieutenant Virtanen from the 1st Battalion, 2nd Field Artillery Regiment, and some five Finnish infantrymen locked themselves in the bunker and continued the battle. Deadly flanking fire from the bunker stopped the 7th and 8th companies of the 733rd Rifle Regiment in their tracks. The Finns tried to counterattack with one infantry company to relieve their besieged comrades in the bunker at 12.00, but this failed. Tovantsev, commander of the 733rd Rifle Regiment, ordered the 9th Company of Junior Lieutenant Beketov to storm and capture the bunker.

The first artillery barrage on the bunker caused it to partially collapse, and men of the 9th Company stormed the bunker at 13.30 for the first time. Lieutenant Virtanen, however, was determined to hold the bunker at any cost. After a pause in communication he resumed radio contact with his battery and continued to coordinate the fire of his cannons. At 14.20 he sent a radio message to his superiors: 'If there is to be no relief, we shall fight until the last man'. Then Virtanen burnt all the papers and prepared to meet his destiny with honour. In a heated battle his handful of men contained the Soviet assaults from the left flank, but on the right flank, at the lake, Beketov's men made their way to the bunker and climbed on its roof. They also brought up several machine guns with them. Lacking any other way of repelling them, Virtanen ordered his battery to fire at the bunker. Several salvoes of shrapnel forced Beketov's men to retreat for a while, leaving the bodies of their dead comrades on the battlefield.

Captain Shevenok's heavy cannons were ordered to target one more barrage on the damaged bunker. A short while later, the left casemate of the bunker and its machine gun were destroyed. The 9th Company approached the crippled bunker again and tried to enter it through a gap in the wall, but Virtanen and his men repelled this assault with hand grenades. The assault was renewed at 18.00, but again Beketov's men were stopped in their tracks by precise artillery strikes called in by Virtanen.

As darkness set in, the Finnish infantry counterattacked at 19.15 and made contact with the besieged garrison at 21.15. Beketov and his men did not give up and assaulted the bunker again, surrounding it late in the evening. The bunker was apparently already empty – the Finns had started the retreat to the second line of defence immediately after making contact with the besieged men inside. The chief-of-staff of the 733rd Rifles, Captain Smetanin, brought in the sappers of the 216th Sapper Battalion, and finally the bunker was blown into pieces at 01.00 on 22 February.

The battle for the last bunker line raged for about a week, with significant casualties on both sides. One good illustration of the ferocity of the fighting is a note made in the war diary of the Finnish Infantry Brigade that was defending the sector: 'the officer losses are so high that there is no one left to write the diary'.

The attacking Red Army units, the 136th Rifle Division and 62nd Rifle Division, were not aware of the last defence line and advanced confidently towards Viipuri, but the advance was stopped in its tracks at the new line of bunkers. The main thrust of the attacking rifle regiments came along the western bank of Lake Muolaanlampi and through a narrow isthmus between lakes Muolaanlampi and Äyräpäänjärvi, where the solitary bunker No. 15 (containing two machine guns) was located, protected by an anti-tank ditch filled with water.

The battle for bunker No. 15 unfolded on 24 February, when the 3rd Battalion, 306th Rifle Regiment, 62nd Rifle Division stormed the bunker with the support of sappers and armour. The Soviet armour was about to surround the bunker, when the Finnish infantry retreated from the trenches around the bunker. The Finnish machine-gun crews of the bunker chose to leave the bunker as well, taking their weapons with them. Second Lieutenant Levanto, artillery observer of the 2nd Battery, 2nd Field Artillery Regiment, was inside the bunker at that critical moment. He kept his head, ordered his artillery observation team to withdraw, and personally led the defence of the bunker with the few remaining men. They opened fire at the attackers using light machine guns and sub-machine guns. The Soviet infantry tried to break into the bunker in every possible way: firing into the gun-ports, detonating small satchel charges, and using Soviet light tanks to fire at the bunker's gun-ports. One of the Soviet tanks was knocked out on the ice of Muolaanlampi Pond, and Levanto managed to kill the escaping crew. In a heated exchange of fire two defenders of the bunker were killed, while another four were wounded.

Eventually, a group of Soviet riflemen managed to throw a satchel charge into the chimney of the bunker. The charge blew the bunker's stove to pieces and the whole bunker was filled with smoke and gas. It was impossible to breathe inside any more and so Levanto decided to break out. It was already dark, and as a result the defenders of the bunker only lost one man killed in the hail of Soviet machine-gun fire that met them as they escaped the damaged bunker. Levanto and his men ran straight into the counterattacking Finnish infantry and joined them in their assault to recapture the bunker. The battle around the bunker lasted late into the night. Soviet sappers used the cover of darkness to bring explosives up to the bunker. Junior Lieutenant Fedorchuk and Sergeant-Major Kuznetsov of the 93rd Sapper Battalion stood waist deep in the ice-cold water of the anti-tank ditch, passing on the explosives towards the bunker, before finally carrying the rest of the platoon across the ditch. Bunker No. 15 was blown up on the same night. The Soviet riflemen and armour poured north, towards Käenniemi hill, threatening to surround the Finnish defenders in the bunkers at Ilves village. Battles zigzagged around Käenniemi until 28 February 1940, but neither side gained the upper hand.

The Finns were desperately short of anti-tank weapons, and the Soviet armour rolled around the battlefield almost unhindered. Flamethrower tanks managed to block one of the bunkers in Ilves village (possibly bunker No. 14) and filled the bunker with burning liquid through the gun-ports, immolating half a platoon of Finnish infantry and a machine-gun section inside. After this incident the garrisons of the bunkers were ready to abandon them at sight of any Soviet tank approaching.

The 3rd Battalion, 378th Rifle Regiment pressed forward against two bunkers east of Ilves village (possibly bunkers nos. 13 and 14) and managed

A so-called 'concrete trench', a cheap concrete bunker from the 1920s, which provided shelter for 5–10 men and a firing step. Two such bunkers were built in the Lähde sector, and were not destroyed by Red Army sappers after the war. (Bair Irincheev)

to reach them in the afternoon of 23 February. The Finnish defenders inside the bunkers refused to surrender. The Soviet battalion had only 100kg of explosives, which did not do any harm to the bunkers. It was late during the night when the battalion at the bunkers saw sappers arrive with a further 500kg. However, the infantry and sapper commanders failed to cooperate; the former withdrew their companies before the sappers were ready to blow the bunkers up. The Finns spotted the withdrawal of the Soviet infantry, counterattacked and forced the sappers to withdraw. When the companies tried to assault the same bunkers, they encountered a wall of machine-gun, mortar and artillery fire from the forewarned Finns. After taking heavy losses and over 12 hours of fighting, the 3rd and 2nd battalions of the 387th Rifles managed to assault and blow up only one of the two bunkers. The battles raged until 28 February, when the Finns withdrew north towards Vyborg. At the end of the battle, the 2nd and the 3rd battalions of the 387th Rifles were down to 30 per cent of their original strength.

The ruins of the Test bunker. Although the bunker had no military significance during the Winter War, its size and formidable appearance drew heavy Soviet artillery fire during the battles in the Lähde sector. (Carl-Fredrik Geust)

Salmenkaita

The story of the fighting in this sector, which raged during the last week of February 1940, to a certain extent repeats that of the Muolaa sector. After withdrawing from the positions at Lake Punnus, the 6th Infantry Regiment defended the sector against the main forces of the 17th Motor Rifle Division. The battles commenced in the sector on 20 February 1940. The 17th Motor Rifle Division had been freshly formed in Gorky (now Nizhny Novgorod) and lacked experience and cohesion, but possessed brave men and commanders. This battle was their main baptism of fire in the Winter War. After several probing attacks it became obvious that the 17th Motor Rifles would deliver their main blow in the middle of the sector with the 278th Motor Rifle Regiment, across Salmenkaita River towards Variksenkylä village.

Several hills covered by forests lie in the fields south of Salmenkaita River. These hills offered superb positions for artillery and their observers. The 17th Motor Rifle Division set all its available regimental artillery to fire over open sights at the hills. Several days later they also received several 8-inch cannons for targeting the bunkers, also over open sights. The commanders of the 517th Motor Rifles Regiment dubbed their hill 'Malakhov Hill', referring to the defence of Sevastopol during the Crimean War against the Western Allies.

The Soviet assault against the Salmenkaita sector started on 21 February 1940. The war diary of the 278th Motor Rifles tells the story of the first attacks:

The enemy fire was relatively weak until our lead units reached an area some 100m from the bunkers. At that point a hurricane opened up from their machine guns and mortars, pinning down our infantry. In the evening the

The remains of the Sj6 'Torsu' command bunker in the Lähde sector. On 13 February 1940 over 20 Finnish wounded soldiers surrendered to the Red Army, after Soviet sappers threatened to blow up the bunker with all men inside. (Bair Irincheev)

political officer of the 1st Battalion, Comrade Senechkin, led the 3rd Company and reached the central bunker itself. However, strong enemy fire prevented other companies from joining them. Left alone at the bunker without any support, the 3rd Company took very heavy casualties during the night. During the first day of battle at the bunker line the 1st Battalion lost about 200 men.

Heavy snowfall in the afternoon and evening of 21 February 1940 provided perfect weather for a scout raid, and the 278th Motor Regiment sent a party of scouts across the Salmenkaita River. The party managed to block and blow up two beach casemates with 17 Finnish soldiers inside, who had refused to surrender. After this the attack on the Finnish main bunker line continued. The war diary of the 278th Motor Rifles takes up the story:

> The weather was not at its best for the assault. It was sleeting, and the men's uniforms and boots were wet. The temperature rose above zero on 22 February. The next day heavy frost returned, with all uniforms, gloves and boots frozen solid. This massively frustrated our assaults … All our attempts to advance and capture the bunkers on 23, 24 and 25 February failed. The regiment suffered significant losses. Many platoon leaders and company commanders were killed or wounded.

The only battalion commander left alive in the 278th Motor Rifles was Captain Vysotski, who wore the uniform of the regular Red Army rank and file, and thus could not be picked out by Finnish snipers. All the local penetrations of the Finnish lines were wiped out by Finnish counterattacks at night. What follows is a description of a dramatic day-long fight for bunker No. 15, as witnessed by a Finnish 2nd Lieutenant who defended it:

A view of the second bunker line in the Muolaa sector. The two bunkers dated from the 1920s, and the anti-tank and barbed-wire obstacles are clearly visible. (Colonel Skvortsov Collection)

> To the commander of the 3rd Battalion, 6th Infantry Regiment. On your orders, I am informing you of the following about our loss of casemate No. 15: I defended the bunker for the whole of 23 February 1940 with my single

machine-gun crew, because, despite my requests to the 8th Company, I did not receive any assistance from them. I only received a message from them that they were not sending anyone to help us from bunker No. 36. Then I sent my reserve machine-gun crew to the ruins of the nearest building, giving them the task of preventing the enemy from climbing onto the roof of our bunker, from which the observation tower had already been shot off. I sent away all men not necessary for the defence of the bunker with this machine-gun crew. By doing so I managed to prevent the enemy's infantry from blowing up the bunker until darkness set in, when the machine-gun crew could no longer clearly see the roof of the bunker. The enemy infantry brought a strong satchel charge onto the roof of the bunker and dropped it into the hole where the destroyed observation tower had been. The explosion of the satchel charge killed or wounded all my men, and when the bunker caught fire, I decided it was time to leave. All the wounded were rescued and received medical treatment. We only left two dead and a destroyed machine gun in the bunker. The machine gun stand and all our equipment were destroyed.

2nd Lieutenant Helmer Honkkila, 3rd Platoon leader, 3rd Machine Gun Company

The same night the Finnish reserve companies counterattacked and recaptured the ruined bunker. The Red Army artillery observers spotted the Finnish bunkers quickly and Soviet artillery rained heavy shells down on them, which immediately inflicted heavy damage. A report by Lieutenant L. Melato (commander of the 3rd Machine Gun Company) to the headquarters of the 6th Infantry Regiment about the condition of the machine-gun bunkers as of 20.00 on 24 February 1940 reveals the ferocity of the battle:

Bunker No 12. The enemy fired on the bunker from 09.00 to 16.15. The observation tower was shot off the bunker at 11.00. The armoured hatches had already fallen down during the previous day. The machine gun carriage is broken. All the doors have been blown away completely. One can see the steel reinforcement from inside the bunker, there are cracks in the ceiling. There are 60cm-deep holes in the concrete roof of the bunker. The lights are completely broken. One machine gun is operational. One rifle has been burnt. The crew is intact. One can stay in the bunker during the night, but not during daytime.
Bunker No. 23. The bunker is operational. Two machine guns are operational.
Beach casemate No. 33. The concrete casemate is operational. The right part of the bunker, made of soil, collapsed on the first day of battle. Two machine guns are operational.
Bunker No. 13. The observation tower has collapsed, the inner doors are broken. The outer door cannot be shut. One machine gun is operational.
Bunker No. 14. The observation tower has been shot off. The part in the corner with the headlight port is beginning to break. One machine gun is operational. There are two captured machine guns at shelter No. 34, both operational.
Bunker No. 15. The observation tower is lying on the ground, the steel door is broken. The wooden parts of the bunker have burnt down. One machine gun was burnt and cannot be used. There are three captured operational machine guns placed in positions around the bunker. The bunker can no longer be used except in emergencies.
Bunker No. 25. Operational. One machine gun is operational.
Bunker No. 16. The inner wheel of the observation tower is broken, and the tower cannot rotate. The doorframe is almost completely broken, as is the frame of one of the gun-ports. The hatch of the headlight port is broken.

The Soviet assaults continued on 26 February and after two days of fighting the Finnish lines were on the point of breaking. The regiment commander requested permission from the division HQ to decide on the moment of disengagement himself. The frontline companies were reporting too many penetrations of the line and the regiment commander was afraid that the division's disengagement order would arrive too late. On 28 February 1940 the Finns withdrew from battered Salmenkaita sector to the north. The final words on the battle of Salmenkaita come from the Finnish officers involved:

> At Salmenkaita the enemy tried to spot our bunkers and their sectors of fire immediately. Enemy infantry managed to close in on our positions under a creeping barrage of artillery, with armour, machine guns and artillery firing simultaneously at our bunkers and their gun-ports. Their infantry marched into battle in close formation, spreading into an assault line only for the final assault. Very often they just walked into battle, under the protection of overwhelming fire superiority. The enemy's infantry did not use rifle fire at all in order to support their advance. The supporting fire of the enemy's automatic weapons was good, especially the machine guns, which were often well placed. The enemy's artillery was extremely active at Salmenkaita, and their marksmanship was good, which was the result of both exceptionally good terrain for observing targets in breadth and depth as well as the calmness of the crews as they were aiming and firing at our bunkers over open sights. The effect of direct artillery fire on the crews of the bunkers was great, the impact on morale was very marked.

Kekkiniemi cannon fort

Kekkiniemi was one of the cannon forts along the northern bank of the Vuoksi River and Lake Suvanto. The fort played a part in the ferocious battle of Kelja in December 1939, when the fresh Soviet 4th Division stormed across Lake Suvanto, taking the Finnish defenders by surprise in the first hours of the 25th. The sector had been quiet up to that point, and the Finnish officers responsible for the defence of the sector were in Christmas mood, largely ignoring reports from the frontline about the Soviet assault. These reports also underestimated the strength of the Soviet task force, mentioning only two platoons crossing the lake, whereas in reality two whole infantry battalions made it across the lake in the morning mist, bringing plenty of automatic weapons with them.

When the Finnish officers woke up to the harsh reality of the situation, the Soviet battalions had already established a bridgehead and cut the road from Sakkola to Terenttilä in the Taipale sector. The Finns brought up two battalions and counterattacked, but this was repelled with heavy casualties for the Finns. The Soviet units on the bridgehead started running into supply problems, as the two cannons of the eastern casemate of Kekkiniemi fort would open rapid fire at any Red Army movement of reinforcements and supplies across frozen Lake Suvanto. The fort itself faced a difficult supply situation, as ammunition and food were not getting through from the rear.

 KEKKINIEMI FORT, ON THE NORTHERN SHORE OF LAKE SUVANTO

This fort played a crucial role in the battle of Kelja between 25 and 27 December 1939. The fort was armed with four cannons, with two each firing in opposite directions. The fort could provide superb flanking fire on the lake and was also very well camouflaged. The two cannons facing south-east prevented the 220th Rifle Regiment from bringing up reinforcements across the frozen lake, forcing the Red Army to withdraw from the bridgehead early in the morning of 27 December.

Kekkiniemi fort, on the northern shore of Lake Suvanto

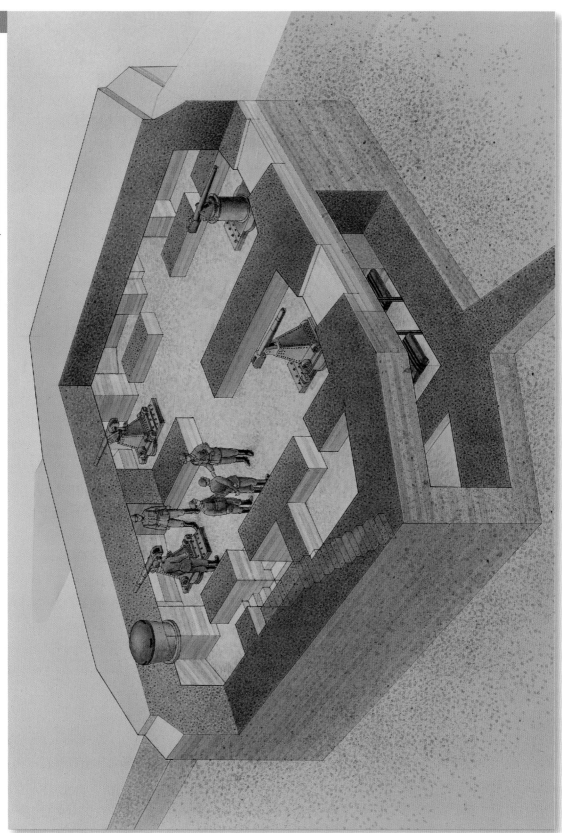

As a result of fire from the fort, the two Soviet rifle battalions on the
bridgehead at Kelja came face to face with the counterattacking Finns. After
three days of hand-to-hand fighting the last Soviet defenders of the bridgehead
were either dead or had been taken prisoner. Finnish losses in reduction of
the bridgehead were also significant. After the Christmas battle the sector
remained relatively quiet for the rest of the war. However, Soviet artillery crews
knew the location of the fort very well and shelled it with 6-inch rounds.
Artillery strikes took place on a regular basis in January 1940. The fort
took numerous direct hits, but the garrison was quick to repair the damage.
The most common repairs comprised strengthening the roof of the fort with
sandbags and logs, as well as digging out the dirt and sand shifted by nearby
explosions. The door of the fort was also blocked by debris on a regular basis.

The garrison was very lucky on 26 January 1940, when the fort took
about 20–30 direct hits from 6 and 8-inch armour-piercing rounds. A 6-inch
shell hit the gun-port of the second cannon, destroyed the log frame, flew
into the bunker, passed through the ammunition box for the Nordenfeldt
cannon, and hit the opposite wall before coming to a halt. Fortunately for the
occupants, the shell did not explode at any point during the journey to its
final destination.

The worst task during these artillery strikes was to be an observer in the
armoured tower. Luckily, the tower did not take any direct hits (it was smaller
and weaker than the armoured towers on the modern bunkers of the
Mannerheim Line), but observers could be hit in the eye with sand and debris,
at least once a day.

The fort held out until the end of hostilities and was still battleworthy on
13 March. In the summer of 1940 it was destroyed with such a powerful

Bunker No. 18 in the Summa Village sector, following its capture by the Red Army. The defences were unfinished when hostilities between the USSR and Finland broke out. Some Finnish officers claimed the armoured towers were shot off the bunkers with ease because the concrete had not hardened sufficiently when the bombardments began. (Carl-Fredrik Geust)

charge that the roof of the fort collapsed. Only a sizeable crater and large chunks of concrete remain of this once formidable fort.

When the villagers from Kelja returned home in 1942, they found a Soviet communal grave in a neighbouring field. The Russian text read that it was the final resting place of 850 Red Army men and their commanders.

Taipale and Patoniemi

The 10 old bunkers in this sector were quickly destroyed or overrun by the Red Army riflemen, and the Finns had to rely solely on field fortifications, which heroically held out until the end of hostilities, despite the best efforts of the Red Army to reduce them. The sector became one of the symbols of the stoic resistance of the Finnish soldiers in the Winter War.

The Red Army units crossed the Taipale River on 6 December 1939, under heavy and precise fire from the Finnish field guns and the Kaarnajoki battery. Shortly after establishing a bridgehead, a Red Army assault party under Captain Netreba captured the mouth of the Mustaoja stream and the three concrete bunkers there. The Finnish counterattacks failed to retake them. The Red Army then prepared for an assault on the Finnish main bunker line.

Mustaoja stream, with its deep, steep valley, became a jumping-off position for the Red Army attacks on the Finnish strongpoints. The weak bunkers, built in the 1920s, were no match for the Soviet heavy artillery and were all out of action by the end of December. From that time onwards, the Finns had to rely on their field fortifications. A massive offensive in mid-December was repelled by the Finns, as was a renewed offensive on Christmas Eve.

January 1940 was relatively quiet, but the Red Army renewed its offensive on 11 February 1940. All the Finnish strongpoints along the frontline were captured and the Finns were pushed some 800–900m to the north from their defence line. Using night counterattacks the Finns managed to regain some of the strongpoints, but were finally forced to fall back due to the overwhelming superiority of the Soviet artillery and air force, and the improved cooperation between Soviet infantry, armour and artillery. The Taipale sector held out until the end of the war, but with heavy losses for the Finnish battalions that defended the sector.

Patoniemi cannon fort lay near to the Taipale sector and was the favourite target of Red Army artillerymen on the southern shore of Lake Suvanto. On 21 February 1940, a heavy Soviet round fired by the artillery of the 150th Rifle Division hit the fort, entered the bunker and exploded inside, detonating around 700 rounds and a petrol tank. The heavily damaged fort was repaired by Finnish sappers later and continued to be used by the Finns.

The rear position around Vyborg

The Red Army reached the outskirts of Vyborg after heavy fighting in late February 1940. The bunkers of the Finnish defence line around Vyborg were all obsolete and very little is known about their military value and the role that they played in the battles. In late February 1940 the problem of the Finnish Army was not fortifications, but rather a lack of reserves and the exhausted state of its frontline soldiers. Losses were accumulating and there was no one to replace the trained troops with. The efficiency of the Finnish defence and counterattacks was slowly decreasing. The coastal batteries at Tuppura and Ravansaari were captured by the Red Army in an assault over the ice with the support of armour; the winter of 1939–40 was so cold that the ice in the Gulf of Vyborg and Finland was over a metre thick, rendering it capable of supporting tanks, gun tractors and other heavy equipment.

ABOVE
A Finnish field cemetery in Taipale, in 1943. Note the battered landscape in the background and the rock wall around the cemetery area. It has become a tradition for every visiting Finn to add a small rock to the wall here. (Bair Irincheev)

RIGHT
Red Army infantry preparing for an assault on the Karelian Isthmus. Note the one-piece camouflaged snowsuit, much more cumbersome than the Finnish two-piece version. The Red Army replaced the one-piece suit with two-piece versions in 1940. (Bair Irincheev)

AFTERMATH

The Finnish Army, which had bravely and efficiently fought the attacking Red Army, was close to collapse in early March 1940. The armistice came at a very good time for the Finns, as a complete collapse of the Finnish defence at the Gulf of Vyborg and in other sectors of the front was only a matter of days.

The Winter War was declared over on 13 March 1940, at 11.00 Helsinki time or 12.00 Moscow time. The armistice had been signed in Moscow the previous day. Finland had to cede the entire Karelian Isthmus and the areas north and east of Ladoga, and rent Hanko peninsula, town and port as a naval base to the USSR. Although Finland remained an independent country, it lost about 10 per cent of its territory. About 350,000 citizens of Finland living in the newly ceded territories had to be accommodated elsewhere in Finland.

During summer 1940 almost all the intact bunkers of the Mannerheim Line were blown up by Red Army sappers. The only ones that remained were too remote or too small to waste explosives on. These bunkers included two old bunkers next to the Terijoki–Koivisto railway in the Humaljoki sector and several other small bunkers, such as the two concrete trenches in the Lähde sector.

The Mannerheim Line became a legendary part of the Winter War, both in the USSR and in Finland. In the USSR, the scale and scope of the Finnish fortifications was exaggerated to a great extent, in order to save the face of the Red Army in the eyes of the public at home and abroad. In Finland, the scale of the fortifications was downplayed; the stoicism and skill of the regular Finnish foot soldier, who defended his country against all odds, was instead stressed.

The Red Army troops that encountered the fortified line for the first time were in awe of the Finnish bunkers. Fantastic rumours, which would seem ridiculous to the modern reader, circulated among those stationed on the Karelian Isthmus. The Red Army infantry was drafted from rural areas with poor standards of education, which fostered the growth of such wild rumours. The most famous one is that there was a thick layer of rubber covering the bunkers in order to deflect incoming artillery shells. The myth emerged after firing at armoured bunkers over open sights. Artillery rounds often ricocheted off, and this gave an impression that a bunker reflected the round as if it were

A view of the formidable Test bunker today. The break in the wall was most likely the result of destruction of the bunker by Red Army sappers during the assault on 11–12 February 1940. (Bair Irincheev)

made of rubber. Other variations of this myth include the belief that the protective armoured plates had springs installed behind them, and that there were special nets that caught and deflected each shell. The latter can be explained by the presence of camouflage nets on most of the bunkers built in the 1930s.

The next myth relates to the size of the bunkers. Red Army political workers vastly exaggerated the size of the Finnish fortifications and claimed the bunkers of the Mannerheim Line were comparable to those of the Maginot Line in France. It was claimed that the bunkers had up to five floors underground, were connected with underground galleries, and had hospitals, power plants, and everything necessary to withstand a long siege. This was far from the truth, as the size of the Finnish fortifications on the isthmus was much smaller than in the Maginot Line. Only a few bunkers that had two floors. No bunkers were connected to each other by underground passages or galleries, nor were there power plants or hospitals inside the bunkers.

Another famous myth is that the Finnish snipers, or 'cuckoos', were positioned in trees. Some Finns did indeed climb up trees, but these were mostly artillery observers and scouts, not snipers. It should be noted at this point that the term 'the White Death' coined by both the Red Army and the Finnish Army most likely refers to the extreme winter conditions encountered, not the Finnish snipers present.

Whatever myths and legends are associated with the Line, it gave both sides an insight into modern siege warfare and fortification design. The new Salpa Line, built by the Finns behind the new Soviet–Finnish border, corrected most of the flaws of the Mannerheim Line. The Red Army, in turn, absorbed the Winter War as an invaluable lesson and embarked on a serious modernization programme, which was interrupted by the German invasion on 22 June 1941.

Generals on both sides studied and analysed weak and strong points of the Mannerheim Line straight after the end of the Winter War. General-Lieutenant Harald Öhkvist, commander of the II Army Corps on the Western Karelian Isthmus, criticized the Line for its high cost of construction and weak firepower. In Öhkvist's opinion, many sectors of the Mannerheim Line that had only field fortifications held off the Soviet attacks with the same success as those with expensive concrete bunkers (the general cited Merkki and Taipale as examples). In his opinion, the bunkers had a formidable strength as passive defences, i.e. shelters, but placing only two or four machine guns into a bunker worth one million marks was a huge mistake. The funds spent on concrete bunkers could have been spent on anti-tank guns, tanks and modern artillery – the key factors in the success of the Red Army.

General Nikolai Voronov, Inspector of Artillery in the Red Army, who was present on the Karelian Isthmus during the assault on the Line, in turn praised the Finnish designers for their skilful use of terrain features, good camouflage and extensive use of interlocking flanking fire, noting 'there was no standard design of concrete bunkers, each bunker was built depending on the terrain and the bunker's mission'. Voronov also praised the Finns for their high standards of tactical and physical training, as well as the excellent marksmanship of individual Finnish soldiers.

In his never-published report, Marshal Kliment Voroshilov, Minister of Defence of the Soviet Union, gave a thorough analysis of the Mannerheim Line plus the strengths and weaknesses of the Finnish and Red Armies, and proposed a whole series of reforms to improve the efficiency of the Red Army. His report in many respects echoed the analysis by Voronov.

In general, the Mannerheim Line earned such an awe-inspiring reputation in the USSR that it became a cliché of the Winter War in general. During the great offensive on the Leningrad Front in June 1944 against the Finnish fortifications on the Karelian Isthmus, the term 'Mannerheim Line' was used again by the Red Army to designate the Finnish VT-Line, which was built between 1942 and 1944.

THE SITES TODAY

All the bunkers of the Mannerheim Line are now on the territory of the Russian Federation. They are not listed as monuments or protected objects of heritage – they stand where they were built and destroyed.

As yet there is no dedicated museum commemorating the Winter War in Russia or in Finland. A small gallery is dedicated to the Mannerheim Line fortifications in the War Museum in Helsinki, while the Artillery Museum in St Petersburg, Russia, has only a couple of artefacts from the Winter War on display.

Some bunkers are easily accessible by car from Vyborg or St Petersburg, as they were built around the main roads. The ruins of bunkers Ink7, Ink6, Sk5, Sk16, Sk6, Mu10 and Mu11 are located right beside the main roads. Other bunkers, some of them with more dramatic histories, are hidden in the forests. Engaging a professional guide who knows their exact location is highly recommended, especially if you visit the Line in the summer months when foliage conceals most of the bunkers.

Munitions were cleared from the ground after World War II, but artillery grenades of all calibres can still be seen on the former battlefields. One must exercise extreme caution as it is highly dangerous to touch or move any such metallic objects, even if they look harmless.

Please note that the Lähde sector of the Mannerheim Line, broken through on 11 February 1940, now forms part of a firing range of the Russian Ministry of Defence. Visiting the site is officially forbidden, but this doesn't stop the locals from going there to pick mushrooms and berries, nor Winter War history enthusiasts from all over the world. It is highly recommended to visit the site only at weekends, when there are no firing exercises. We also highly recommend you check the announcements of the 138th Guards Motor Rifle Brigade on the community billboards in the nearby villages, in case of extraordinary exercises on weekends.

The largest bunkers of the Mannerheim Line still have some inner chambers preserved. These are the bunkers Ink6, Sk2 'Terttu', Sk11 'Peltola', Sk10 'The Ten', Sj5 'Millionaire', Sj4 'Poppius', Le6, Le7 and Su4. Access to some of the inner chambers is complicated. In general, we recommend you visit bunker Sk10 'The Ten' – both the entrance and exit from the underground gallery are easy and relatively safe. A good flashlight is a must, and a protective helmet is highly recommended. Please note that sometimes you can encounter bats inside the bunkers. If you visit the bunker line in the summer, please beware of swarms of mosquitoes and flies. A mosquito net is highly recommended especially, in June and July.

There are several Finnish-based travel agencies that run tours to the area, among them JaPi matkat (www.japimatkat.fi), Lomalinja (www.lomalinja.fi) and Bair Travels Oy (www.bair-travels.com, run by the author of this book). The latter runs the tours in Finnish, Russian and English, while other travel companies provide guides in Finnish. Bair Travels Oy runs both individual and group tours in the area.

A Finnish memorial on top of a wooden dugout in the Summa village sector that was destroyed on 21 December 1939 by a direct hit from a heavy shell. All 19 men inside were killed. They were all from the village of Kalvola, not far from Hämeenlinna, which led to the memorial being named the Cross of Kalvola. (Bair Irincheev)

BIBLIOGRAPHY

PRIMARY SOURCES
Finnish Military Archives (Sota-Arkisto), Helsinki
Russian State Military Archives (RGVA), Moscow

SECONDARY SOURCES
Anonymous, *Talvisodan historia 1–4* (Gummerus, WSOY, 1977)
Anonymous, *Boi v Finljandii* (Publishing House of the People's Commissariat of
    Defence of the USSR, Moscow, 1941)
Antero Uitto, *Carl-Fredrik Geust Mannerheim-Linja – Talvisodan Legenda*
    (Gummerus, Jyväskylä, 2006)

FURTHER READING
Philip Jowett and Brent Snodgrass, *Finland at War 1939–1945*, (Osprey Publishing,
    Oxford, 2006)
Sami Korhonen, www.winterwar.com
William Trotter, *A Frozen Hell: The Russo-Finnish Winter War of 1939–1940*
    (Algonquin Books of Chapel Hill, 1991)

APPENDIX: THE MANNERHEIM LINE SECTORS

Sector	Old MG bunkers	Old shelters	New MG bunkers	New shelters	Modernized MG bunkers	Cannon forts	Total
Kaipiala	3	3	-	-	-	-	6
Närjä	7	1	-	-	-	-	8
Römpötti	5	3	-	-	-	-	8
Näykki	3	3	-	-	-	-	6
Kolkkala	7	5	-	-	-	-	12
Humaljoki	4	-	-	-	-	-	4
Inkilä	-	-	7	-	-	-	7
Kolmikesälä	6	6	-	-	-	-	12
Karhula	5	2	-	-	-	-	7
Summankylä	4	5	3	1	4	-	17
Lähde/ Summajärvi	2	6	2	-	-	-	10
Leipäsuo/ Äyräpää	5	-	2	-	-	-	7
Suurniemi/ Muolaanjärvi	-	-	5	2	-	-	7
Muolaa	4	7	11	-	1	1	24
Salmenkaita/ Mälkölä	4	1	18	3	-	-	26
Lauttaniemi	2	-	-	-	-	1	3
Noisniemi	2	-	-	-	-	1	3
Kiviniemi	2	-	-	-	-	1	3
Sakkola	2	-	-	-	-	1	3
Kekkiniemi	2	-	-	-	-	1	3
Patoniemi	2	-	-	-	-	1	3
Taipale	8	1	-	-	-	-	9
TOTAL	**79**	**43**	**48**	**6**	**5**	**7**	**188**

Sectors in the rear position around Vyborg

Sector	Old MG bunkers	Old shelters	New MG bunkers	New shelters	Modernized MG bunkers	Cannon forts	Total
Lyykylä	2	-	-	-	-	-	2
Heinjoki	1	2	-	-	-	-	3
Nuoraa			-	-	-	-	
Kakkola			-	-	-	-	
Leviäinen	18	1	-	-	-	-	19
Ala-Säiniö			-	-	-	-	
Ylä-Säiniö			-	-	-	-	
TOTAL	**21**	**3**	**-**	**-**	**-**	**-**	**24**

INDEX

References to illustrations are shown in **bold**. Plates are shown with page and caption locators in brackets.